I0814399

Meet Me at Luke's

Lessons in Life and Love from Gilmore Girls

KRISTINE ECKART

Illustrated by Laura Marr

Andrews McMeel
PUBLISHING®

Contents

Luke's
MOBY DICK
A Tale of Two Cities
The Hunchback of Notre Dame

The Dragonfly Inn

INTRODUCTION

Welcome to Stars Hollow

"It's a lifestyle."
"It's a religion."

—Lorelai and Rory Gilmore (Sn 1 Ep 14)

Every season is *Gilmore* season, but now more than ever is the perfect time to celebrate our friends in the greatest small town in the world. Created by Amy Sherman-Palladino, *Gilmore Girls* premiered in October of 2000. Twenty-five years have passed since the pilot aired, since that first moment when we pulled up a chair at Luke's Diner and joined Lorelai and Rory Gilmore for coffee. Whether you've been a dedicated fan for every one of those years or have more recently discovered the show, I'm thrilled to welcome you to this celebration! Regardless of your own Gilmorean journey, your affection for the show, books, or pop culture has led you to these pages, where we will honor what began as a simple mother-daughter series and transformed into a phenomenon that touched the lives of countless viewers. Consider this book a literary Stars Hollow festival, brimming with a cozy atmosphere and plenty of *Gilmore* magic.

Gilmore Girls has undeniably captured the hearts of audiences through its witty, rapid-fire dialogue, the irresistible appeal of its small-town backdrop, and its remarkable ability to provide insights into our own lives. The show's impact is staggering—according to Nielsen, the company responsible for tracking television ratings, viewers dedicated an astonishing 586 million minutes to watching *Gilmore Girls* September 2–8, 2024. Of course, the amount watched fluctuates monthly, but for a yearly estimate, that would total almost thirty billion minutes, an astronomical figure that truly emphasizes the show's widespread appeal. Netflix also reports forty-five million views of the show from July to December 2023, contributing to the show's placement in the Netflix Top 10 for the year, revealing that current *and* new viewers are spending time watching the show every day.

It's not difficult to imagine fans willingly spending another thirty billion minutes immersing themselves in the world of Lorelai and Rory; the devotion of *Gilmore Girls* fanatics knows no bounds. Their passion is palpable as they eagerly tune into *Gilmore*-themed podcasts, proudly display coffee mugs adorned with the iconic Luke's Diner logo, eagerly absorb interviews with the show's stars, embark on pilgrimages to the actual Connecticut town that inspired the fictional setting, and even permanently ink themselves with the inspiring motto of the Life and Death Brigade: *In omnia paratus.**

Dedicated fans repeatedly rewatch the entire series, a beloved ritual and testament to the show's enduring allure and the comfort it provides, no matter how many times we experience it. Like millions of other *Gilmore* addicts, I consider myself an honorary Gilmore girl. I've adored the show since its debut on the WB, and I've revisited Lorelai and Rory countless times since. I've rewatched episodes so frequently that I can recite the dialogue as quickly as Lorelai herself! The Gilmore girls have been a part of my life for over a decade—their most recognizable quotes naturally find their way into my daily conversations, while their insights on movies, TV, food, and books influence my decisions. When the autumn leaves begin to fall, and the air becomes cool and crisp, I turn to the Gilmores. During chaotic times, when I'm feeling lost or lonely, I find solace with the Gilmores. They comfort me on bad days, and we celebrate together on the good days. For me, all roads lead to *Gilmore Girls.*

* Rory translates this to "ready for anything," but it can also mean "prepared in all things."

There aren't many TV shows that I associate with such precious memories. However, *Gilmore Girls* stands out from what feels like billions of hours of TV I've watched because the series added another layer of fellowship to the significant relationships in my life. My friends and I eagerly discussed what happened on the show every week, setting aside Tuesday nights as dedicated *Gilmore* nights. (The show's first season aired on Thursday nights but switched to Tuesday nights in the second season.)

I still remember the excitement and grief I felt during the final episode. My sister, two of our friends, and I were all ardent fans, but our Tuesday night choir practice abutted the *Gilmore* air time, ensuring that we'd miss the cold open and maybe the first scene while rushing home from church. Usually, that was fine, but we were dead set on watching every second of the finale. We left choir practice a few minutes early and rushed back to our friend Katie's house (which was closest). Together, the four of us watched as all of Stars Hollow wished Rory "Bon Voyage." Because streaming wasn't a thing then, watching a show as it aired was a big deal. You couldn't just catch it later; either you saw it or you didn't, making the experience more memorable and exclusive. Just like Lorelai and Rory had their little inside jokes that reinforced their bond, we had *Gilmore Girls* to give our friendship one more memorable aspect that connected us.

Gilmore Girls resonates with many fans because of its idyllic mother-daughter focus, and I feel the same way. Inevitably, this show was also a part of my bond with my mom (and I'll share more details in the next chapter). Although I'm sure she watched the show with us while it was on air, I don't recall it being a dedicated "mother-daughter" thing until years later. Several years ago, when we were on a family vacation, I needed some quiet time to rest. My room in our Airbnb was a basement den, so I settled back on my bed/couch and queued up *Gilmore Girls* to help me relax. A few minutes later, my mom came downstairs and sat with me to keep me company. Watching TV together is such an ordinary thing, but it's moments like these, where loving companionship quietly shines through, that make this simple act extraordinary.

Still, as much as I hold this show and its characters dear, I never imagined they would shape my life so profoundly and universally. I never envisioned the Gilmores becoming my guides, modern-day Virgils leading me through life's circles, but that's precisely what they've become. In 2018, I launched the *Gilmore Book Club* blog, creating a space for friends and fans to discuss the more than four hundred books referenced in the show, along with all the other delightful aspects of the characters' trials and tribulations. Since then, I've immersed myself in the world of *Gilmore Girls*, growing my digital community and engaging with fans from around the globe.

Like Chilton was the pathway to get Rory to Harvard, the *Gilmore Book Club* blog was my bridge to becoming an author. My blog is no *Norton Anthology of Theory and Criticism,* but it was a testament to how pop culture could create community and change lives. It helped fans connect over who was "Team Jess," gave them a platform to discuss works like *The Holy Barbarians* and *The Children's Hour,* and celebrated the little moments of *Gilmore*, like the discovery of a coffee-scented candle, that bring joy to our lives. Writing about the intricacies of the show and the influences of pop culture for the blog, I discovered so many insights on how *Gilmore Girls* shaped the person, the woman, the friend, and the writer I am today. If Lorelai and Rory had transformed my life for the better, I was sure they'd do the same for others.

This book was my way of taking this life-changing experience to the next level by sharing it with the world and helping the benefits of these life lessons reach as many people as possible. That's right, you're about to get a crash course on the transformational teachings of *Gilmore Girls*. This journey is a fan-led experience: all inferences and lessons learned are my own, as well as any mistakes. So, put on your walking shoes, *Working Girl,* and turn your baseball cap backward because we are going back to Stars Hollow.

And what a remarkable group of friends we'll have by our side! Babette and Miss Patty will insist on sharing overly intimate details. Luke will serve up coffee with a side of curmudgeonly perspective on love. Sookie will offer unwavering loyalty and mouthwatering baked goods. Lane will help us understand the profound role of music in life. Paris will assist us in overcoming life's obstacles, and Kirk will guide us in finding our purpose.

Naturally, Lorelai and Rory will remain our most steadfast companions. They'll always have an ample supply of obscure cultural references, junk food, and advice on mother-daughter relationships. Lorelai will guide us in finding our home and encourage us to stay true to ourselves. Rory will demonstrate how reading can transform our lives and show us the significance of creativity. Finally, with Richard and Emily, we'll delve into the Gilmorean philosophies regarding privilege, finances, and parenting styles. It's quite a journey, but don't worry–I'm a fast talker!

My deepest hope is that something within these pages resonates with you and helps you on the rest of your journey. You don't need to spend *A Month of Sundays* 📖 scanning for the *Gilmore* spirit in stacks of books or the shows' episodes as I have to benefit from the life lessons of the Gilmores. (However, you're welcome to do as much reading and binge-watching as you like.) Like Max Medina, I believe in sharing our stories, so this book will share all the *Gilmore Girls* life lessons I've learned. It aims to provide the comfort of wrapping yourself in a blanket for a movie marathon, coupled with the gentle guidance and occasional tough love of a friend who nudges you toward becoming the best version of yourself–a true Gilmore at heart.

However, just like Taylor has to leave instructions with his dish donations, I have a few things to address before we dive in. If you appreciate spoiler warnings, here they are: We'll be delving into every season of *Gilmore Girls* from start to finish. So, if you have yet to see every episode, proceed with caution to avoid spoilers! I'll primarily focus on the initial seven seasons and skim over most of *Gilmore Girls: A Year in the Life* (*AYITL* for short), which aired nine years after the original show. Plus, the original Rory Gilmore Reading Challenge (that so many fans are undertaking) focuses on books from the first seven seasons, so I think it works out nicely for the book and for the twenty-fifth anniversary to focus on the original series, the original reason we all fell in love with *Gilmore Girls*.

Similar to the show, this book will overflow with pop culture references. If you're worried you'll feel like you're attending a town meeting where Lorelai references *Norma Rae* and nobody catches it, fear not! I've done my best to surround each reference with enough context clues to help you understand what I'm talking about without calling Nancy Drew. However, just as Rory tells Jess to figure out why she calls him "Dodger" after he steals one of her books, I'm encouraging you to look up these references yourself so you can fully understand and appreciate the nuances of each. As Richard Gilmore says, "We learn something every day," and I hope you take that idea to heart as you continue to read *Meet Me at Luke's*.

Like Rory, I have a list for everything, so at the end of the book, you'll discover a comprehensive list of cultural references spanning movies, music, food, and literary allusions that contribute to the show's greatness. Whenever you encounter a book title marked with this symbol [ ], you'll know that it's part of the official Rory Gilmore Reading Challenge book list, which is also in the back of this book, along with more *Gilmore* checklists and resources. (Curious about how many *Gilmore* books you've read? Turn to page 199 to find out!) *Gilmore Girls* also produced a prodigious Gilmore Movie Challenge list! Those titles will be marked with this symbol [ ], and the directory of those references starts on page 200. Basically, if you read this book, you'll have the pop culture repertoire of a Gilmore in no time.

So, keep those Pop-Tarts within reach and your coffee well stocked as we embark on a walk-and-talk stroll down memory lane in the company of *Gilmore Girls*.

Copper boom, Gilmore!

Timeline of Major Plot Points in *Gilmore Girls*

Before we jump into the life lessons, let's refresh our memories on the pivotal moments from the show. Many of these will be referenced in later chapters and will serve as the foundation for the lessons we're about to discuss.

Season 1

- Pilot (Episode 1): Rory is accepted to an elite *Old School* institution, a.k.a. Chilton Preparatory School! Willing to make a Faustian bargain to help her daughter, Lorelai reaches out to her estranged parents to help pay the tuition. In return, Lorelai and Rory must have dinner with them every Friday night.
- Episode 8: Lorelai's first date with Chilton teacher, Max Medina, is full of fiesta burgers and romantic walks in the snow.
- Episode 9: Rory and Dean make it official after some not-so-romantic reading of Dorothy Parker's poetry.
- Episodes 16–17: Dean builds Rory a car (NOT like the one in *Christine*) and says he loves her; Rory completely blanks, and they break up.
- Finale (Episode 21): Max proposes to Lorelai with a thousand yellow daisies and the best proposal speech ever; Rory finally says "I love you, you idiot" to Dean.

Season 2

- Episode 3: Lorelai realizes Max isn't "the one" and calls off the wedding.
- Episode 10: The Bracebridge Dinner, Jackson in tights, and Rory riding in a horse-drawn sleigh with Jess! *Old Christmas* but make it Stars Hollow.
- Episode 13: Dean and Jess (Luke's nephew) battle over a picnic with Rory at the Bid-on-a-Basket fundraiser.

- Episode 19: Rory and Jess get into a minor car accident. Jess flees the scene—and Stars Hollow.
- Finale (Episode 22): Sookie and Jackson get married! Rory kisses Jess (he's back!). Plus, Lorelai sleeps with Christopher, but their relationship hopes are dashed when Christopher finds out his girlfriend, Sherry, is pregnant.

Season 3

- Episode 7: Rory and Lorelai participate in the Stars Hollow Dance Marathon, but Rory's breakup with Dean eliminates them from the competition.
- Episode 9: Rory and Jess (whom Emily likes to call *Lord Jim* 📖) are officially dating now.
- Episode 16: "The Big One"! Rory is accepted to Harvard, Princeton, and Yale.
- Episode 17: The Independence Inn catches fire, and the town rallies around Lorelai and Sookie. Plus, "Babette Ate Oatmeal" and "Faux Poes 📖 Foes."
- Finale (Episode 22): Rory graduates from Chilton! Lorelai and Sookie buy the Dragonfly Inn. Rory reinstates Friday Night Dinners with Richard and Emily to help pay for Yale.

Season 4

- Episode 2: Rory moves into her Yale dorm room and discovers she's living with a new and improved Paris. Go, Bulldogs!
- Episode 9: The Harvard vs. Yale game brings it all out: Richard still has lunch with his college girlfriend, Pennilyn Lott; Lorelai goes on a date with Richard's business partner, Jason; and Paris is making out with a sixty-year-old professor. It's all very *Peyton Place*. 📖
- Episode 11: Lane's band, Hep Alien, has a gig at CBGB in New York, but it turns into a fiasco that ends with Mrs. Kim kicking Lane out of the house.

- Episode 18: Richard's old boss announces he's suing Richard and Jason and reveals Lorelai and Jason have been secretly dating for three months. Oy with the poodles, indeed.
- Finale (Episode 22): The Dragonfly invites Stars Hollow's townies for a test run. Lorelai and Luke kiss, finally! Rory sleeps with Dean, who is married to Lindsay–yikes!

Season 5

- Episode 1: Emily announces she and Richard are splitting up. Emily and Rory pull a *Daisy Miller* and go to Europe for the summer to escape their troubles. Lorelai and Luke start dating.
- Episode 6: Norman Mailer, Sookie's pregnant!
- Episode 8: Rory and Dean break up . . . again. Rory sets her sights on Logan Huntzberger, or *Master and Commander,* as he likes to be called.
- Episode 13: Richard and Emily are back together and renewing their vows. Christopher's interference breaks up Luke and Lorelai. Rory almost hooks up with Logan at the wedding.
- Finale (Episode 22): Logan's dad, Mitchum Huntzberger, crushes Rory's journalistic hopes. Then Logan and Rory steal a yacht. After their arrest, Rory decides to drop out of Yale. Lorelai spontaneously proposes to Luke.

Season 6

- Episode 1: Luke and Lorelai are engaged! Rory begins to understand her *Crime and Punishment* and is sentenced to three hundred hours of community service. She also moves in with Richard and Emily and is no longer speaking to Lorelai.
- Episode 2: Paul Anka (the dog) joins the Gilmore family. He's no *Lassie* or crazy *Cujo,* but he is afraid of peas and porch steps!
- Episode 9: Rory returns to Yale and reunites with Lorelai.
- Episode 12: Lorelai finds out Luke has a daughter with his ex-girlfriend. Luke convinces Lorelai to postpone their wedding.

- Episode 19: Lane and Zack tie the knot and have two ceremonies. "Praise Buddha!"
- Finale (Episode 22): Lorelai begins to think her wedding to Luke may never happen.

Season 7

- Episode 1: Luke and Lorelai officially call it quits, breaking the hearts of fans around the world.
- Episode 4: Lorelai starts to date Christopher, and their *Funny Face* 🎬 movie date is interrupted by Emily calling to say she's been arrested.
- Episode 7: Lorelai and Christopher elope in Paris—au revoir single life, bonjour to "Mr. and Mrs. Hayden."
- Episode 12: Lorelai helps Luke win custody of his daughter, April, and Christopher interprets this as Lorelai's unresolved feelings for Luke. Richard has a second heart attack.
- Episode 21: Rory is preparing to graduate from Yale, and Logan thinks that's the perfect time to propose.
- Series Finale (Episode 22): Rory turns down Logan's proposal and gets a job as a journalist on a presidential campaign. The town of Stars Hollow comes together to say goodbye to Rory, during which Luke and Lorelai are reconciled. It's time for one last coffee at Luke's before we say goodbye.

Luke's
Ne
Neon
What she
TACKLES
she
CONQUERS
Ca
Calcium
A+
NABOKOV

STARS · HOLLOW
to Hartford
The Dragonfly Inn
Miss Patty's
Dance Studio
Doose's Market
STARS HOLLOW BOOKS
HARDWARE
Luke's
TAYLOR'S SODA SHOPPE
Luke's Diner
WESTON'S BAKERY
The Gazebo
Stars Hollow High
Kim's ANTIQUES
Sookie's
The Independence Inn
Lorelai and Rory's

The Divine Secrets of Monkey, Monkey Underpants

How to Fully Show Up in a Mother-Daughter Relationship

"Thank you, Mom, you are my guidepost for everything."

—Rory (Sn 3 Ep 22)

From interpreting each other's dreams about oil vats to sharing makeup, clothes, and CDs, Lorelai and Rory's unique bond offered a new way for mothers and daughters to relate to each other. But what makes their connection so special? True, Rory and Lorelai are closer in age than most mother-daughter dyads, which does help the friendship aspect of their relationship, but it's only one contributing factor. It's their communication style and unending devotion that put them in a category all their own.

Lorelai Gilmore is a departure from the two kinds of moms that previously appeared on our TV screens. The first is the absent or semi-absent mom. These characters had either passed away, such as the Halliwells' mother on *Charmed,* or were not a significant part of the storyline and therefore seldomly appeared to give maternal advice, like Jo from *Lizzie McGuire*. I'm not saying these were bad or intentionally absent mothers; they were just less present in the show's plot. Then, you have the traditional mothers like Debra from *Everybody Loves Raymond* 🎬 and Kitty from *That '70s Show*. These moms put food on the table for breakfast and dinner, cared for the house, and kept the family unit running smoothly.

While these maternal character types offered care, love, and advice for their children in different ways, they were always in parent mode. Perhaps some may have wanted to be best friends with their kid, but no child on TV would ever permit that—until the Gilmores came along. Lorelai and Rory's "friends first" attitude and their ability to talk about the details of their lives and feelings with real intimacy changed the mother-daughter dynamic on television, altering how viewers began to see their relationships with their own mothers and daughters.

Gilmore Girls is famous for its fast-paced dialogue, pop culture references, witty puns, comedic bits, and comebacks for just about everything. Yes, the Gilmores do a lot of talking, and this habit is most apparent—and most remarkable—when it comes to Lorelai and Rory. They talk about everything: the good, the bad, and the just plain weird (like when they debated the grammar of "culs-de-sac").

Lorelai and Rory's constant communication is the bedrock of their relationship. It's not just a way of passing information back and forth like a box of Pop-Tarts; it's a way of repeatedly solidifying their bond. Their conversations cover it all: friendships, experiences, topics, thoughts, and ideas that, inside *and* outside of the TV world, a mother-daughter duo might not share. It's the talking we associate with best friends, sharing the most secret thoughts on things like kissing the prep school bad boy at a party and dreams of being an international news correspondent or running their own inn.

However, their talking serves another purpose. The Gilmores' rapid pace, pop culture–laden references, and inside jokes create a unique language that only their closest friends (and lovers) can begin to understand. For Lorelai and Rory, this creates a world that is theirs alone, one that exists inside their exclusive mother-daughter bubble.

When Lorelai became a mother, she decided to prioritize her friendship with her daughter. She rarely "plays the mom card," like when she insists that Rory not tell Emily about the termites eating at their house.

Emily Gilmore's outlook is different. According to her upbringing and the ethos of her class, the purpose of the mother-daughter relationship was not friendship; it was for the parent to mold and guide the child. There are a few friend-adjacent moments for Emily and Lorelai—like when they stole the bathrobes at the spa. More often than not, however, their relationship is like when rival groups the Greasers and the Socs try to hang out together 📖; it will only end in disaster. Emily believes she can help create the best life for Lorelai, so she interferes with Lorelai's household, relationships, and career. Emily orders DSL internet to be installed without Lorelai's permission and sets Lorelai up on a blind date during a Friday Night Dinner. It may be a misguided way to interact with her daughter, but Emily does all of this because she loves Lorelai and wants the best for her. However, actions like these are what initially prompted Lorelai to leave her parents' house and move to Stars Hollow, causing a rift that plagued the Gilmores throughout the series.

I don't think Emily's approach is healthy for any relationship, let alone with a strong-minded, opinionated, and independent person like Lorelai, but that's Emily for you. Somehow, the void between Emily and Lorelai only deepens when Lorelai tries to improve their relationship. Lorelai's attempts at sharing her "Vicious Trollop" lipstick with Emily or inviting Emily to see Stars Hollow fall apart each time, and she knows their inability to communicate is the source of the problem. They express themselves often enough, but not in a way the other person can understand.

Lorelai and Emily need to find a language they can share, and until they do, they'll be stuck in a state of distrust and conflict, just like Lane and

Mrs. Kim (which we'll discuss more in the chapter on parenting). If Lorelai and Emily found a way to express their thoughts and feelings without simultaneously attacking the other person, their relationship might be different. In traditional Gilmore fashion, though, they don't talk about Lorelai leaving home at all; they let that wound fester until it explodes in season six's "Friday Night's Alright for Fighting," where they air their grievances and start to understand how the other is feeling and their relationship begins to heal.

Words bind us all together. From casual banter to heartfelt discussions about our world, all those words weave together to create stories and relationships. And words are an integral part of my connection with my mom. When it comes to talking, my mom and I have a very Gilmore relationship—we often use Lorelai's "monkey, monkey, underpants" line as a transition during our conversations. It's also rare that I intentionally don't share something with her. As a teenager, when I was out late, she'd stay up to ensure I was safely home *and* to hear my version of events from that night. These conversations were more than just a quick rundown of events. They held details of my inner thoughts and emotions that other kids would have left out of their "mom packets."

Gilmore Girls' emphasis on talking is so important that it's part of the show's tagline: "Life's Short. Talk Fast." However, there's another thing we rarely look at when it comes to Lorelai and Rory, something that, over the years, I've learned to pay more attention to: the silence.

There are times when we go all *Terms of Endearment,* with Shirley MacLaine screaming at nurses, but there are also times when words fail us. When we're tongue-tied or can't express our thoughts because we can't even comprehend what we're thinking, words begin to slip away. And just like that, we're left in silence.

In season three of *Gilmore Girls*, Rory dates the controversial James Dean–like Jess Mariano. Millions of *Gilmore* fans may be Team Jess, but Lorelai fluctuates between Anti-Jess and Tolerate Jess. One night, Rory comes home and tells Lorelai she is thinking about having sex with Jess. True to her monogrammed towels, Lorelai plays it cool. But on the inside, she's totally taken aback at this very adult topic that she didn't even know was on Rory's mind. This moment marks a vital shift in their relationship, one that could take Rory farther away from Lorelai, emotionally and physically, and that scares them both.

There will be many tests like this for their relationship in the future, but now, Lorelai must decide whether she wants to know everything about Rory's life, even if it makes her uncomfortable. However, Lorelai could also determine that she'd rather not know the most private details of Rory's thoughts and feelings and try to preserve the same relationship they previously had. One day, Rory will also have to choose to continue sharing her innermost secrets with Lorelai and hearing Lorelai's secrets in return, but for now, the choice rests with her mom. Lorelai's mom gene eventually overpowers the awkwardness, and she chooses her bond with Rory over her own comfort. And so, their relationship passes into a new phase without eroding. Rory is growing up, but so is Lorelai.

After they agree to still discuss everything despite their discomfort, they sit on the couch and eat their dinner, contemplating this change in their lives and working to find their sea legs aboard this next stage in their relationship. It's a moment of profound love and silence.

I know what you're thinking: Lorelai and Rory, silent? It's rare, but it happens! To sit in such an uncomfortable moment after a difficult conversation, nervously looking into the future but choosing to stay by someone's side anyway, is a physical display of loyalty. It's an act of "thick love," as Toni Morrison would say, an act inspired by only the deepest and most devoted love.

These shifts happen in all our relationships, but choosing to grow and adapt is crucial to sustaining our connections. My mom and I have had to adjust too. When I was a teenager, I was diagnosed with a chronic illness that led to a profusion of doctor visits and an annoying amount of time in the car driving to all the various appointments. For most of this, I was exhausted and in pain, which meant I could only sit in the car with my eyes closed, wishing I'd fall asleep but unable to do so. My mom was *Driving Miss Daisy* for hours and hours in silence.

With the disappearance of my verbal abilities, my relationship with the world and those around me began to dissolve. Even the most minuscule words were agony, costing me precious energy I couldn't afford to lose. But my mother knew what I was only beginning to comprehend: that relationships require equal amounts of language and action.

My mom loved me in all the ways she knew how, despite my silence. She continued to care for me and drive me to multiple appointments for multiple doctors. No matter how quiet, sick, difficult, or lost I was, she never abandoned me. She always let me know that she was there for me, never allowing my lack of communication to affect our relationship. As her daughter and her friend, I hope I do the same.

What we say to each other matters, and finding that special shared language can create an incredible Lorelai–Rory-type bond. Your language might be discussing *The Wisdom of the Ancients,* making up new dialogue for your favorite TV shows, or debating whether "How 'bout that schnitzel?" is a punch line. Whatever it is, make sure that your communication style benefits the relationship. But don't forget that actions can also speak volumes. Showing up, in good times or bad, can make or break a relationship. That's why investing your time is a fundamental part of a mother-daughter connection. Whether it's to sit in comfortable silence or do something as simple as walk through town, companionship can help sustain the magic and love in a mother-daughter relationship.

Life's short–show up and talk, Gilmore!

Behind the Scenes: How the Gilmore Girls Were Cast

Gilmore Girls depended on the mother-daughter relationships in the show, so finding the right actors to play Emily, Lorelai, and Rory was vital to creating the series.

Alexis Bledel was working as a model when her manager convinced her to audition for the role of Rory Gilmore in a pilot. Alexis nervously showed up to the casting session with a bad cold, and even though all she wanted to do was lie down, she read the lines. While Alexis felt unsure about the whole thing, Amy Sherman-Palladino saw Rory come through that day and wanted Alexis badly, even though Amy felt sure Alexis didn't like her. Thankfully, that wasn't true. And so, the first Gilmore was cast.

The search for Lorelai Gilmore was more difficult. Amy Sherman-Palladino recalled at the 2015 ATX Television Festival that she kept skipping over Lauren Graham's headshot because Lauren was working on another show and was unavailable. Amy didn't want to fall in love with someone she couldn't have. Lauren, however, read the script and said she knew she was meant to play Lorelai because "she couldn't stand the thought of anyone else doing this [role]," a notion inspired by Christopher Reeve on *Inside the Actors Studio*. As luck would have it, Lauren could get away for a few hours to talk to Amy and read some lines. Lauren was cast immediately and, thankfully, released from her other commitment.

Kelly Bishop, who plays Emily Gilmore, had the same experience many other actors do: she showed up and auditioned. Kelly remembers thinking, "I own this woman [Emily]. I know who she is." Her certainty in the character was evident, and everyone saw it, except for some reason they didn't tell Kelly. As much as she loved the script, Kelly told herself to forget about the project because she hadn't heard any response from her audition. Only later did her agent get answers from the production team, and they said, "Oh yeah, she has the job!"

And thus, the Gilmore girls were born.

Top Mother-Daughter Moments

The Perfect Shot

Coffee and a burger at Luke's is the quintessential Gilmore aesthetic, but it all started in the pilot episode with Lorelai and Rory doing what they do best: talking and eating. The final shot in the episode celebrates this mother-daughter bond in an iconic way as the camera captures a close-up of Lorelai and Rory in Luke's Diner and then slowly pulls back to frame the Gilmores through the diner window. The final episode of the final season pays homage to this special moment by re-creating the same scene of Lorelai and Rory sipping coffee as seen through the diner window, cementing the beginning and the end of the show in the magic of this mother-daughter relationship.

Season 1 Episode 1 "Pilot" and Season 7 Episode 22 "Bon Voyage"

"The Incredible Sinking Lorelais"

Nothing causes a Gilmore to break down more than being unable to talk it out. When Lorelai is overwhelmed by renovating the Dragonfly and Rory feels like she's failing at Yale, they both desperately need the comfort of the most important relationship in their lives. However, just as all the plans *Of Mice and Men* usually go awry, their busy lives and conflicting schedules prohibit them from conversing. This episode depicts that Lorelai and Rory's bond is strengthened by their ability to communicate. Still, when they can't verbalize their thoughts and feelings to the one person who is always there for them, their mental state begins to suffer. But no Patty Hearst moments here: Luke comforts Lorelai, Dean consoles Rory, and our Gilmore girls go on to conquer what they tackle.

Season 4 Episode 14 "The Incredible Sinking Lorelais"

One More

No one follows *Robert's Rules of Order* like Mrs. Kim, so it's understandable that she has to close all the curtains and lock all the doors to pull out the alcohol she's hiding on the top shelf. Mrs. Kim knows that

Lane's current crankiness is caused by her breakup with Zack, which also forced Lane to move back home. Apparently, Mrs. Kim's approved way to grieve and move on is to do some mother-daughter shots. Bottoms up at the Kim house!

Season 6 Episode 11 "The Perfect Dress"

We Own Windmills

We owe the discovery of the Gilmore windmills to Lorelai helping Emily with her taxes. After several training sessions on navigating and managing Emily and Richard's finances, Emily can "click, click, click." However, she's still not confident she can manage everything alone while Richard is on a sabbatical and feels like she's the only one paddling their life canoe. So, Emily uncovers the hidden liquor–no more mocktails–and she and Lorelai share a moment of vulnerability and admiration for each other as they talk about their lives with their spouses. Emboldened by how well she and Emily are getting along, Lorelai reveals that she and Christopher have split up and is relieved when Emily comforts her instead of criticizing Lorelai about the breakup. Here's looking at you, kayak. 🎬

Season 7 Episode 15 "I Am Kayak, Hear Me Roar"

MACBETH
Shakespeare
To Kill a Mockingbird
The Secret Life of Bees
Mrs Dalloway
THE GODFATHER
PUZO
OUT of AFRIC
DENNISON
PLATH
HAPPY
IRTHDAY
FEZ
A Tale of Two Cities
DICKENS
Carol
CD
H
Y
Tales
THE GREAT GATSBY
TREE Grows In BROOKLYN
HAROLD and the PURPLE crayon
THE COMPLETE POEMS
ANNE SEXTON
Atonement
QUATTROCENTO
MCKEAN
ROOSEVELT
HIGH FIDELITY
HORNBY
THE SUN ALSO RISES
Deenie
BLUME
Holidays on Ice
Stories By DAVID SEDARIS
HOW THE LIGHT GETS IN
HYLAND
BELOVED
Morrison
Wuthering
HEIGHTS
BRONTË
NORTHANGER ABBEY
AUSTEN
EMMA
AUSTEN
A SEPARATE PEACE
Bel Canto
ANN PATCHETT
NIGHT
ELIE WIESEL

Bring a Book to Sniff

How Reading Can Change Our Lives

"I live in two worlds. One is a world of books."

—Rory (Sn 3 Ep 22)

In Rory's season three Chilton valedictorian speech, she describes the magnitude of her literary world, reminiscing about her adventures "aboard the Pequod and strolling down *Swann's Way.*" It is perhaps one of the most famous quotes from *Gilmore Girls* and certainly one of the most beloved. It's referenced in Bookstagram captions, recited by fans, and written on the side of one of Rory's favorite bookstores, the Strand, in New York City. With her endless passion for books, Rory Gilmore is a cultural and literary icon, a celebration of what it means to be a bookworm and how books can transform your life.

However, Rory isn't the sole source of the compendium of *Gilmore* literature: Lorelai, Richard, Emily, Paris, and Jess all contribute bookish references with their dialogue or can be seen reading various tomes throughout all seven seasons. Even Mrs. Kim, who normally sticks to reading the Bible, likes to mix things up a bit and mystifies Dave in season three with quotes from Shakespeare's *Henry VI.*

Literature is central to the ideology of a Gilmore. Creator Amy Sherman-Palladino said she wanted these characters to be well rounded, knowledgeable, and invested in the world around them—and the literary references do just that. With each mention of Pushkin, Dostoevsky, or *The Canterbury Tales,* the Gilmores instill a level of colorful cleverness that brought the banal daily tasks in their lives to another level.

TV often stereotypes scholarly characters as nerds; just look at *The Big Bang Theory*. Other main characters are created with a more approachable, charmingly normal lifestyle, like in *The Office* or *How I Met Your Mother,* but lack an elite level of brilliance. The Gilmores were different. Intellect and wit were their way of life, but in a manner that was cool and attainable, and all you had to do was open a book.

However, the Gilmore bibliophilia didn't just make them fun to talk to at parties; it sustained them. It transformed them. What does Richard do after discovering his business partner was suing him? He reads *Points of View.* While coping with Trix's slanderous letter, Emily dives into *The Crimson Petal and the White.* When Lorelai felt restless and misunderstood in her childhood, she turned to books on travel and music. And Rory, well, she reads just about everything in response to, well, everything.

Stories reflect who we are, depicting all the definitions of what it means to be human, which is why books mean so much to so many people. Books are a "uniquely portable magic" (Stephen King), a "form of prayer" (George Saunders), a mirror in which "you only see . . . what you already have inside you" (Carlos Ruiz Zafón), something that "schooled you in ways that school couldn't" (Monica Ali), and a tool that helps you "gain a sense of . . . [yourself] in the world" (Maya Angelou). All of that is true, but the one thing I have discovered in literature is its ability to transform.

I know Max Medina can be a controversial character, but I believe he said it best.

I have studied and taught the great literature all my life, and those stories are replete with characters that let opportunities slip by. But what I teach is more than just literature. It's lessons and life. If I don't follow the tenets of those lessons, I'm not the man I thought I was. The man I want to be.

—Max Medina

Literature, lessons, and life are all inextricably linked. Books give you the foundation, the plan, the experience, the road map, or, if you live in Stars Hollow, the egg map. All of life's adventures, even those you could never have encountered yourself in a million years, such as creating a living man out of chopped-up body parts, are painstakingly detailed for you to absorb as if they were your own history.

However, literary transformation is not guaranteed. It is accessible only to those willing to think about these literary messages and act on their experience. Think of it this way: reading about a character making a good or bad decision in a book and failing to respond in your own life is just as bad as knowing you have gunk in your teeth and doing nothing about it, maybe even worse.

The Gilmores know how to take the lessons in books and use them to their benefit. Richard, who dedicates years to reading tomes like *The Outbreak of the Peloponnesian War,* *The Fall of the Athenian Empire,* and biographies on Molière, is a man who is unfalteringly devoted to his goals and will pursue them despite the ups and downs of his career. He credits his creativity to *Richard III* and *Macbeth,* and his cunning is evident in his business dealings. When Richard is unhappy with his job, he leaves and starts his own company. When that company is in trouble, the Gilmore patriarch bags a better deal with his former employer. His eye is always on the prize. Thanks to his literary upbringing, he knows how to observe a situation and use it to his advantage.

Rory, despite her intellectual heritage from her grandparents and mother, is often the one most guilty of ignoring the wisdom of books, which drives me bonkers! When we first meet her, Rory is an incredibly bright sixteen-year-old on the cusp of brainy brilliance. No one would contend Rory's academic acumen, but I will argue that she didn't use her wisdom in the most beneficial way, but we get to learn from her oversight.

Mr. Medina taught his students that learning from books was more than regurgitating the answers on a test about dates, symbols, and archetypes. It was about learning from the experiences, discussions, and emotions in those books and applying them to your own life. We all know that Rory can make a sizeable pro-con list, but she often ignores her emotions. She fails to connect her life experiences with what she has learned in her extensive reading.

Hold on to your Cletuses and Desdemonas, because I'm about to lay out some radical questions. If Rory had really understood *Anna Karenina,* would she have slept with Dean even though he was married to Lindsay? If Rory had studied all that *Moby-Dick* meant, would she have stolen a yacht? If she had taken *The Vanishing Newspaper* and *My Life as Author and Editor* to heart, would she be the transient, unfocused person we reunite with in *A Year in the Life*? And now for the big one: if Lorelai had married Max, would he have been able to teach Rory how to apply all the knowledge from books to her own life so she wouldn't have gotten into any of these messes in the first place?

We will never know what could have been, what mistakes and heartbreak might have been avoided in the lives of the Gilmore girls, though perhaps we can hope for a better future. All we can do is be aware of the vast world of knowledge in books and apply it in our lives. We may not always get it right—I sure don't—but I'm willing to bet that if you do, it will pay off.

For most of my life, I have read like Rory. Ever since I was little, my universe has been filled with books and imagination. It didn't matter that the other kids were playing tag, because I was more interested in whatever world I was visiting, whatever adventure I was undertaking, or whomever I was meeting in the pages of a book. So, it's no surprise that I turned to books, *Gilmore Girls*, and the Rory Gilmore Reading Challenge when I needed something more.

With over four hundred stories, the Rory Gilmore Reading Challenge is not for the faint of heart. While some entries on the list are plays like *Death of a Salesman* and, therefore, faster to read, others are quite extensive, like *The History of the Decline and Fall of the Roman Empire,* which is over 1,900 pages. For reference, that's almost twice the size of *Nicholas Nickleby,* the Gilmores' favorite book to reference when something is incredibly long, and some books on this list are not as entertaining as one would hope. Nevertheless, I decided to read them all.

Initially, I was reading as Rory did in the show, going through book after book just to check it off a list. I wasn't reading as Rory *should* have been reading—like Max Medina tried to teach his students to read. Maybe I had been subconsciously taking in some of the lessons from *Great Expectations* or *Beowulf,* but I certainly wasn't doing it intentionally.

Then, one day, Scarlett O'Hara's voice was going 'round and 'round in my head like a literary Energizer Bunny. Then Elinor Dashwood and Colette chimed in, and I knew these stories were more than just safe havens or entertainment. They were guides, imaginary little Yodas materializing in and out of my brain at seemingly random times. Each one was there to tell me something. From then on, I began to look at my life and the books I was reading through a different lens and opened my mind to what literature was trying to teach me.

Sometimes, the message was clear: *David Copperfield* told me to hang in there and keep working, and *Jane Eyre* kept reminding me to discover who I am before engaging in a relationship. I know that seems simple, but when your life feels like *An American Tragedy,* some comforting *Tuesdays with Morrie* little life lessons can feel really good. While marrying a wealthy suitor is never more appealing than when you're skint, a read of *Madame Bovary* will show you there are drawbacks to marrying just for money.

Books don't just invite you into their world, though; they bring their world into yours, opening your eyes and mind to ideas and experiences you could never have imagined. What the characters feel, you feel; what they discover, you discover. Within the pages of the book, however, there's an end for them. You get to keep going. You get all the wisdom of a hero's journey without the battle scars. You get to turn your story around.

Your actions could have unforeseen consequences, but books will help you play those scenarios out and make the best-educated prediction possible to continue on your journey.

While our trials may not be the same as others', and our paths are different, the steps are similar. No one gets to walk through life completely unscathed. I'm incredibly blessed, but I have endured my share of anguish and life-altering encounters: financial worries, sexual discrimination, medical problems, dashed hopes—you name it. But books and the Gilmores have taught me that I always have a choice: I can choose to keep blundering ahead, or I can open a book, just as Jess embraced learning from that *You Deserve Love* nonfiction book in season five. I can use what I learn to make a better way forward. And not just *any* way forward—the way that works best for me and me alone, the path that will lead me to my most genuine and best self.

Books help us escape, recharge, question, understand, dream, live, and heal. I will always need that, and many of you will too. As Rainer Maria Rilke advises, "Live a while in these books, learn from them what seems to you worth learning, but above all love them. This love will be repaid you a thousand and a thousand times."

Every word in every book plants a tiny seed, and those seeds take hold in your soul to give you what you need. Literature allows us to grow in unexpected places, like a mighty tree flourishing in concrete instead of soil—an emblem of resilience and strength. So, start to read like Rory 2.0: interpreting books using Max Medina's approach by merging the lessons of literature with your life. Use the experiences and words of wisdom found in books to transform your life, to thrive, and to be your best, most authentic self.

Keep reading, Gilmore.

Top Books Everyone Should Read from the Rory Gilmore Challenge According to Kristine

Challenging yourself to read all of the four-hundred-plus books on the official list can be overwhelming; don't worry, you're not alone. I'm just like Rory, standing in front of the Harvard library, almost hyperventilating about the books I haven't read yet. But please, no hyperventilating, quitting before trying, or negative self-talk. I've compiled a list of my favorite books from the Rory challenge so you can start your reading journey with the best of the best.

Kristine's Favorites *

- *Divine Secrets of the Ya-Ya Sisterhood* by Rebecca Wells
- *The House of the Spirits* and *Eva Luna* by Isabel Allende
- *The Lord of the Rings: The Fellowship of the Ring, The Two Towers,* and *The Return of the King* by J. R. R. Tolkien
- *The Secret Life of Bees* by Sue Monk Kidd
- *A Tree Grows in Brooklyn* by Betty Smith
- *Atonement* by Ian McEwan
- *Pride and Prejudice* by Jane Austen
- *A Tale of Two Cities* by Charles Dickens
- *Macbeth* by William Shakespeare
- *The Godfather* by Mario Puzo
- *Wuthering Heights* by Emily Brontë

* When the book icon appears in the section title, all books listed are from the Rory Gilmore Reading Challenge.

If you're in a reading slump or unsure about the whole reading thing in general, it helps to start with a short book. So here is a list of my favorites from Rory's list.

Favorite Short Books

- *To Kill a Mockingbird* by Harper Lee
- *Ella Minnow Pea* by Mark Dunn
- *How the Grinch Stole Christmas* by Dr. Seuss
- *The Great Gatsby* by F. Scott Fitzgerald
- *A Christmas Carol* by Charles Dickens
- *A Room of One's Own* by Virginia Woolf
- *Letters to a Young Poet* by Rainer Maria Rilke

It's OK to have a love-hate relationship with literature. Some parts of a book can really resonate with you, while others repulse you as much as Taylor's annual tick talk. (Can you imagine the nausea of Taylor's tick talks if he were on TikTok? Yuck! But I digress.) Being able to hold that juxtaposition in your mind and body is clearly a part of Stars Hollow, but also a part of life and of literature. So here are the books that would earn an "it's complicated" relationship status on my literary rankings page.

"It's Complicated" Books

- *The Devil in the White City: Murder, Magic, and Madness at the Fair That Changed America* by Erik Larson
- *Bel Canto* by Ann Patchett
- *Out of Africa* by Isak Dinesen
- *The Song of Names* by Norman Lebrecht
- *A Mencken Chrestomathy* by H. L. Mencken
- *A Brief History of Time* by Stephen Hawking

The literary world of the Gilmores extends into the real world through the Rory Challenge and the Gilmore cast members themselves, who have created works of art and linguistic walks down memory lane to add to your bookshelf.

Books of Gilmore Cast and Crew

Lauren Graham

- *Someday, Someday, Maybe* (2013)
- *Talking as Fast as I Can: From Gilmore Girls to Gilmore Girls (and Everything in Between)* (2017)
- *In Conclusion, Don't Worry about It* (2018)
- *Have I Told You This Already? Stories I Don't Want to Forget to Remember* (2022)

Keiko Agena

- *No Mistakes: A Perfect Workbook for Imperfect Artists* (2018)

Shelly Cole

- *Blue Highways* (2022)

Stan Zimmerman

- *The Girls: From Golden to Gilmore* (2024)

Kelly Bishop

- *The Third Gilmore Girl* (2024)

Nick Holmes

- *Time Spent Falling* (2016)
- *Downpour* (2019)

Rosebud Wallpaper

How Lorelai's Scarlett O'Hara Mindset Can Help Us Find Home

"I'm going to be without a home . . . I mean a *home* home—a memory home."

—Lorelai (Sn 2 Ep 8)

If you were to look at the collage of images above my desk, you'd find a sketch of a blue two-story house with a white wraparound porch cozily surrounded by trees. This image, of course, is a drawing of Lorelai Gilmore's house in Stars Hollow, a place that is not only Lorelai and Rory's home but also a representation of the home so many fans have found in *Gilmore Girls.* I've placed Lorelai's house right in my eyeline so that it's the first thing I see when I look up from my desk, a designated spot of honor, to remind me of everything the Gilmores have taught me about life and finding my home.

The idea of home is a constant theme in the show, starting with Lorelai's discomfort at living with her parents in Hartford—our first illustration of the concept that home isn't just the place where you live. Or, as the season five finale title tells us, "A House Is Not a Home." How true that is. The combination of her parents and their lifestyle meant that

Lorelai never felt at home during her childhood, something that must have affected her profoundly and informed her decisions as she grew up.

The disconnect between a house and a home has an immeasurable influence on one's psyche and sense of safety. We see the repercussions of this disconnect in Lorelai's rebelliousness and strict adherence to the rules that keep her parents out of her life. Lorelai may not carry noticeable scars like Ethan Frome, but she does bear the invisible wounds from when she felt like she didn't belong. As a result of living with Richard and Emily, Lorelai doesn't trust that good things can come from a place of love instead of a place of manipulation and expectation of repayment, so she picks fights when she gets scared and uses humor to avoid having serious conversations. Just like Lorelai, I have scars of my own.

I, too, grew up constantly feeling out of place. This is not to say that I had a bad childhood or wasn't cared for; it just means I never belonged in my hometown. My diffident demeanor hindered my ability to make friends, and my preference for more sedentary activities like reading separated me from what other kids wanted to do. My physical childhood house was a place of refuge and fun, but it was also a reminder of a world where I didn't fit in, like *Stuart Little* in a world of humans. Everyone around me was obsessed with football, and I wanted to read books like *The Kitchen Boy.* As Richard observes in season six, "You can live somewhere your entire life and never truly feel at home," and that's how I felt about South Carolina. Perhaps this is why Lorelai and I are so physically and emotionally attached to our current dwellings; we feel at home only when we're fully allowed to be ourselves, a notion I've only recently begun to understand.

I've been fortunate enough to live in many places. My apartment in Chicago was one of my favorites for many reasons; my Los Angeles place, not so much. But New York is the city I've called home for most of my adult life. I shared my first apartment here with a roommate I had known since I was little. We got along incredibly well, and I enjoyed living there, but when she got married, it was time for me to move out.

Anyone who has ever lived in New York knows it's the worst place to find a home. New York is the third major US city I've lived in, and nothing has prepared me for the maelstrom that is trying to find an apartment here. There's not only the issue of finding a new place, hopefully beating out the other eager renters, but also filling out extensive applications, interviewing to live there, packing up your current home, and moving everything. And, of course, every step of this process costs an exorbitant amount of money, which, if you're just starting in your career, is a significant cause of stress. Moving is never easy, but as fate would have it, I was going through this process at the worst possible time.

Back then, I worked for a lingerie sales agency, and twice a year, we took all the brands we managed to a big expo show at the Javits Center, coincidentally right where Liz Danes shows off her jewelry in *Gilmore Girls.* These shows take massive amounts of planning, prepping, and packing–and I coordinated it all. During the month before the show, I dealt with all sorts of issues at work and home every day, trying to get these gigantic projects done simultaneously. You've heard of Murphy's law, right? Well, things can and did go wrong. Each day brought up new problems, and I was a complete wreck trying to deal with it all. So much so that one day, after discovering a few more hoops I had to jump through, I had to give myself a time-out in the bathroom because I couldn't stop the tears from rolling down my face. The more days that passed, the more impossible everything became.

So, there I was, barely holding it together and still getting up every morning to do it all over again, just like how I imagine Lorelai must have felt after she left her parents. My mind was a chaotic jumble of to-do lists, deadlines to meet, and upcoming problems, but one of Lorelai's Scarlett O'Hara–inspired statements kept coming to mind: "I'll think about it tomorrow," an intentional procrastination that prioritizes essential tasks and preserves one's sanity.

Moving day was unfortunately also the same day as the expo event. While I went to work, my parents, with the help of my friends, moved my small truckload of belongings to my new apartment. (Can you tell I have the best parents?!) They finished packing my boxes, drove everything to the new place, unloaded, and set up the essentials—all without me. I woke up in one apartment and slept in another that night; it was entirely surreal.

My parents left the next day. I was moved into my new apartment, and the work event was over, but that didn't mean everything was fine. Exhausted and incredibly sick, I had no energy to clean up anything or unpack any of the numerous bags and boxes stacked around my apartment. Think Lorelai's living room when she's accepting all the donations for the town rummage sale—total chaos. Each day, I rummaged through suitcases looking for clothes and shoes or cooking utensils but couldn't find what I was looking for. I think I called my mom at least once a day for the next few weeks so she could help me locate things I was missing. On top of that, I felt sad about leaving the previous apartment and my roommate; I had no sense of closure or transition between places, and I felt guilty that I hadn't helped with the move. My new dwelling was full of clutter, sickness, and negative feelings, and I resented it for not being the home I wanted it to be.

As the weeks went on, however, nothing I did brought me closer to that feeling of "home." People would ask how I loved my new apartment, and I always lied, adopting Lorelai's fake smile. "The community there is so wonderful," I'd say. "It barely feels like I've moved at all." All these things were true, technically, but they were only platitudes that covered up my true feelings.

What makes a house a home? I think home is a place that reflects the life you want to live. It's a haven full of love and joy, your own peaceful *Walden* retreat when you need comfort and rest. As much as I wished for my new apartment to be that home, I couldn't figure out how to manifest that vision into reality until I thought of Lorelai.

While many may not consider a potting shed a nice place to live, it was the place Lorelai and Rory called home when they first came to Stars Hollow. This simple ramshackle shed sat on the edge of the grounds of the Independence Inn, where Lorelai initially asked for a job after she left her parents' home.

Years later, when Rory takes Emily to see the potting shed, Rory describes her time there with such love and the nostalgia that makes the Gilmore girls sparkle. Emily, horrified at their floricultural abode, runs away faster than a *Marathon Man.* I doubt Rory's affinity for the shed is related to its proximity to gardening tools; we all know the bulb disaster of season four and the subsequent flip-out are likely the extent of the Gilmores' relationship to nature. So, what is it about the potting shed that Rory remembers so fondly?

The potting shed is Lorelai's first opportunity to make her mark and set up her life, and she uses what she has to the best of her abilities. She puts up lovely rosebud wallpaper and floral artwork to make it bright and beautiful. She sets up a curtain around the bathtub to create a faux bathroom and brings in old furniture from the Independence Inn to make the entire space more comfortable. The fact that Rory remembers their time there fondly and calls it her favorite place is a mark of how much love and care Lorelai poured into their home.

Lorelai gave the same Gilmore treatment to the house they finally moved into after the potting shed, filling Rory's room with all the books she could want, snagging some spare furniture from the inn, and adding her quirky style to every room with strange clown pillows, a monkey lamp, and a cow napkin holder. Just like Scarlett fought to make Tara a home again, Lorelai fought to make their first house, and their eventual blue house, a home, not just for Rory but for herself too.

If Lorelai can HGTV makeover a potting shed, why couldn't I transform my apartment? So, I resolved to do just that. I'd take one thing at a time and go from there. I focused on something Lorelai made an effort to have in their first home: the shower curtain. I spent a ridiculous amount of time on the internet searching for just the right one, but my endeavor soon turned into something requiring a Goldilocks-grade level of decisiveness. After standing in my bathroom and staring at the first shower curtain for longer than anyone should, almost willing it to be what I wanted, I decided it was too dark for the space and sent it back. I had high hopes for the second option I ordered, but that, too, wasn't right. Was I being ridiculous? It was, after all, just a shower curtain. However, I had vowed to do everything in my power to make this place my home. I was going to fight for my home, and a part of that was fighting for the perfect shower curtain, darn it!

Thankfully, the third shower curtain was just right! I know this is not the most pivotal decor in one's home, but I loved that shower curtain. Even though there were still boxes to open, shelves to organize, and areas to clean, every time I walked into my bathroom, I saw that shower curtain and felt like I had finally been able to take that first step to make my apartment into my home. I could finally see a future in my apartment. I could finally see myself reflected in my home.

Of course, other places can become our home too. Our relationships, careers, and hobbies also become our homes because we pour our hearts into them. And when we do, they reflect who we are–the good and the bad. But we'll get into finding all of these other homes in other chapters.

Lorelai helped me to see that what makes home so special is how much time and effort we've dedicated to that space, how much passion we fill it with, and how much love we share when we are there. All of those things require patience and hard work. And with time, the memories that enhance one's special bond with one's abode will come and make one's time there even more extraordinary. It's an *Odyssey*, to be sure, but that journey will make everything worth it in the end.

We all need that home, but home isn't just anywhere. It's where you feel accepted and at peace. It's where you can revel in the joy and recover from your wounds. You may have to work to make it the home you've dreamed of, but when you do, you'll realize that you belong to that place just as much as it belongs to you.

Welcome home, Gilmore.

The Real Stars Hollow

Sadly, Stars Hollow is not an actual city, but it does exist on the backlots of WB Studios in Burbank, California. However, a lot of TV magic went into making the set look like a real small town. Here are a few of my favorite TV magic tricks and secrets about the *Gilmore Girls* sets, courtesy of Warner Brothers BTS videos and *Gilmore* Key Set Costumer Valerie Campbell's insider information.

- "The Jungle," also known as where Luke pushes Jess into the lake, is actually an artificial forest with a concrete ditch. When water is needed for the scene, the ditch is filled, and the bridge/pier is moved in and out as needed.
- All that fluffy snow was really mashed potato flakes. Yum!
- The trees in the town had removable leaves so that production could change them in and out for each season. However, all the plants and flowers you see at Emily and Richard's are real.
- The bushes on the Gilmores' patio hid the craft service department (the very important crew that makes food for everyone), which was directly behind that set.

- The Gilmores' pool house was re-created to also serve as Rory and Paris's off-campus Yale apartment.
- Luke's apartment isn't actually above Luke's Diner. His apartment set was across the street in the firehouse.
- The Wilshire Ebell Theater, an off-the-WB-lot location, served as the set for DAR meetings, the Bangles concert, Emily and Richard's vow renewal, Rory's cotillion, and the Chilton formal dance.

I hope I didn't spoil the magic of Stars Hollow for anyone with this information.

Academy Award–Winning Movies Mentioned in *Gilmore Girls* 🎬

It's movie night at the Gilmores'! So, grab your popcorn and enjoy a significantly edited version of Rory and Lorelai's favorite Oscar-winning movies. (Remember, a more complete list of Gilmore movies is in the appendix.)

An American in Paris (1951): Best Picture, Best Screenplay, Best Cinematography, Best Art Direction, Best Costume Design, Best Original Score

Breakfast at Tiffany's (1961): Best Original Song, Best Original Score 📖

Camelot (1967): Best Art Direction, Best Costume Design, Best Original Score

"We can never see *Casablanca* together. . . . I don't care how much I love it, but I will not be responsible for ruining *Casablanca*."

—Lorelai (Sn 7 Ep 4)

Casablanca (1942): Best Picture, Best Director, Best Screenplay

"So, you're going to live forever? Like on *Fame*?"

—Sookie (Sn 2 Ep 1)

Fame (1980): Best Original Song, Best Original Score

Fiddler on the Roof (1971): Best Cinematography, Best Sound, Best Music

From Here to Eternity (1953): Best Picture, Best Supporting Actor, Best Supporting Actress, Best Director, Best Screenplay, Best Cinematography, Best Costume Design, Best Sound, Best Film Editing

Gigi (1958): Best Picture, Best Director, Best Adapted Screenplay, Best Cinematography, Best Art Direction, Best Costume Design, Best Film Editing, Best Original Song, Best Musical Score

The Godfather (1972): Best Picture, Best Actor, Best Adapted Screenplay

> **"I thought you loved *The Lord of the Rings*. You said you wanted to see it one hundred times!"**
>
> —Dean (Sn 2 Ep 15)

The Lord of the Rings: The Return of the King (2003): Best Picture, Best Director, Best Adapted Screenplay, Best Film Editing, Best Art Direction, Best Costume Design, Best Makeup, Best Original Score, Best Original Song, Best Sound Mixing, Best Visual Effects

Mary Poppins (1964): Best Actress, Best Film Editing, Best Visual Effects, Best Original Song, Best Original Score

The Music Man (1962): Best Musical Score

My Fair Lady (1964): Best Picture, Best Actor, Best Director, Best Cinematography, Best Art Direction, Best Costume Design, Best Sound, Best Musical Score

Roman Holiday (1953): Best Actress, Best Story, Best Costume Design 

Sabrina (1954): Best Costume Design

Seven Brides for Seven Brothers (1954): Best Original Score

Sophie's Choice (1982): Best Actress 

The Sound of Music (1965): Best Picture, Best Director, Best Film Editing, Best Musical Score, Best Sound

To Kill a Mockingbird (1962): Best Actor, Best Adapted Screenplay, Best Art Direction

West Side Story (1961): Best Picture, Best Supporting Actor, Best Supporting Actress, Best Director, Best Cinematography, Best Art Direction, Best Costume Design, Best Sound, Best Film Editing, Best Musical Score

Don't Squander the Gift of Fish

Knowing and Achieving Your Purpose

"What if that's my calling, the thing that I'm meant to do?"

—Lorelai (Sn 3 Ep 12)

Did you know that you could have the miraculous gift of fish, and you're wasting your time doing all that other stuff? OK, let's be honest; the gift of fish is something Lorelai jokes about having only when she's trying to learn to be an angler from a book and then from Luke (in Sn 3 Ep 12), but the scene does have a real-life element that is very important: finding your purpose.

From asking what children want to be when they grow up to inquiring about someone's career, our culture is obsessed with purpose, but we tend to use this word only when discussing our jobs, and this topic is so much more than that. Let's be clear: your job is *not* your "reason for being." Purpose is an all-encompassing passion and destiny that gives your life meaning. So, how do we dive into this existential purpose pickle? We ask the Gilmores, of course. Before we begin, I want to clarify that we're talking about each character's purpose in their own lives, not their purpose on the show.

Emily Gilmore may be the series' most straightforward representation of purpose; the rest of the characters can be somewhat murky or fluctuate throughout all seven seasons. (None of these approaches is necessarily right or wrong when it comes to purpose; it's just that character's path.)

From the moment we are introduced to Emily Gilmore, her objective is Baccarat crystal clear: to be the support system (for her husband) and a guide (to her daughter). She was born and raised for this role, and she believes in this duty with every fiber of her being. For Richard, she's there to plan the business parties, maintain their social connections, and guarantee their household runs smoothly. For Lorelai, Emily deems that she is there to help her socialize with the right people, develop the persona that fits their world, and provide a household commensurate with her status.

For those reasons, Emily is also a great example of one who knows their purpose early on and rarely strays from that path. (I'm one of those people, too, and like Emily, I can get a little extra crazy about my passions for that reason.) However, Emily also portrays society's definition of purpose. Her future was planned at a young age, and she knew she was never going to use her history degree; she was going to be a wife and mother. There's nothing wrong with either of those roles except that Emily didn't deliberately choose them for herself.

There are only a few instances where Emily's purpose comes into question. The first, and one of the biggest, is Lorelai's departure from home at sixteen, citing the stifling environment at the Gilmores' as part of the reason for her escape. In season four, Jason cancels the routine business launch party in favor of an unconventional trip to Atlantic City, which implies that Emily's treasured vocation of planning parties is "stuffy and out of date." Season four also shows Emily finding Trix's letter that begged Richard not to marry Emily right before their wedding, and Emily begins to question her marriage, something she thought was rock-solid. And in season six, Rory moves out of the pool house, giving Emily some serious déjà vu flashbacks to when Lorelai first left.

These moments throw Emily's life off-kilter, and until order is restored, she is out of sorts to the level of wearing a bathrobe during the day. For many years, Emily and Lorelai avoid discussing Lorelai's teenage emancipation, allowing their differing opinions on their life's purpose to disrupt their relationship. For the other scenarios, focusing on how she cares for Richard helps recover Emily's equilibrium. Making sure Richard gets the first pick of all the appetizers at Trix's wake allows her to resume her wifely duties, and she begins to feel like herself again. As we can see, when you're not connected to your purpose, your entire life seems unfocused and out of balance.

Richard Gilmore is usually a provider and protector. He gets up early and goes to work, making deals and making money to provide his wife and daughter a quality life. His role as father to Lorelai tends to take a back seat to his other position as the breadwinner. Still, he is also more flexible in his definition of what a dad should be, so his relationship with Lorelai tends to be less volatile than Lorelai's relationship with Emily. But it's also because of this role that we see Richard yelling at Mitchum Huntzberger and Straub Hayden (Christopher's father), suing Jason, and, in one of the most brilliant scenes ever, planning a *Sting* operation with Rory to prank Logan in season five. Richard is usually even-tempered, but when anyone threatens his family, he transforms into a Liam Neeson–inspired guardian who will go to the ends of the earth to protect those he loves.

The funny thing about finding your purpose is its intrinsic requirement of both intention and discovery; you have to purposely pursue it, but you also have to leave room for the unexpected that could change everything. Emily and Richard have an absolute vision of who they are meant to be and use that to craft their destinies deliberately. But only some have such a clear and precise vision of life. Even with all of the luck in the world, I'd venture to say that many people still have to work at finding what they're meant to do. But don't worry, we'll talk about how to invite such fortune into your life and use it to your advantage.

That brings us to another group of *Gilmore* characters: those who had no idea what to do with their lives and found their destinies by chance.

What else would you call Lorelai's journey other than kismet? The baby she was never supposed to have became her world, motivated her to create her own life, and helped her discover one of her best roles: motherhood. The inn she may have never visited became her "memory home," livelihood, and inspiration for her next passion: owning her own inn with Sookie. Two of Lorelai's most important raisons d'être were orchestrated by happy accident.

Only after giving birth to Rory and working at the Independence Inn did Lorelai find her purpose and begin to live intentionally to ensure the continuation of those dreams. I want to be specific: Lorelai's purpose is not "mom" and "inn owner." Her purpose is to take care of others and give them, even temporarily, a loving, comfortable home. That was the most significant thing missing in her life with Emily and Richard but something she found at the Independence Inn and with Rory. Lorelai even lives this purpose in other ways: feeding and taking care of Lane, having biweekly lunches with Paris, giving Hep Alien their first place to practice, and allowing Kirk to spend several nights at her place when he leaves his mother's house. Whether at the Dragonfly Inn, at her house, or by offering her presence, she finds her purpose in giving people a home.

There's also Lane, whose *What Color Is Your Parachute?*–type job assessment reveals she should be in sales; however, it's only when a music store happens to open in Stars Hollow that Lane sits down at her first drum set and discovers her destiny is to inspire others with music.

Of course, as with anything measured on a spectrum, there are examples of finding purpose that range between intention and experimentation. Early in season one, Rory reveals that she wants to pursue journalism. We don't get a definite reading of the *why*, but the viewer can glean some inspiration behind Rory's career choice. She's a good writer, even maybe an excellent one, earning praise from Chilton's newspaper faculty advisor, so we can conclude that Rory's purpose might be sharing stories.

Perhaps not having a clear purpose behind her journalism endeavor is why she allows tempest Mitchum Huntzberger to blow her so far off course, the real reason behind Rory quitting Yale. Maybe his condescending conversation with Rory telling her she "doesn't have it" just magnifies the self-doubt she already feels in her abilities and her purpose.

Any good book or class on writing, business, or life will ask you *why* you want to do something. Yes, we all need money to put food on the table, but if money or fame is your only motivation for wanting something, it's not a good enough reason.

So, how did the Gilmores help me find my destiny? In this instance, the Gilmores worked their magic through the Rory Gilmore Reading Challenge, directing me to the book that would show me my purpose.

I have always wanted to be a writer. I was so enamored with books as a kid, and on one magical day, when I realized that someone out there was creating these books, and that was an actual vocation, I knew I was meant to be an author. For many years, I would have said my purpose was to share stories with the world, but looking back now, I see that it wasn't specific to me; it didn't include the one thing that only I could do because of my unique voice and experiences. And because of this, I, too, had

"Rory years" where I wasn't writing a lot and I let others tell me my voice wasn't good enough.

I was back on track with my writing when I picked up *The Power of Myth* by Joseph Campbell (edited by Jackie Kennedy) ; that's also one of Paris and Rory's favorite ways to spend spring break. My first time reading this book, I was gobsmacked to see the path of my life so clearly laid out by a deceased professor who didn't know a single thing about me. Campbell's hero's journey is very detailed, so, here's the quick version, starting with how I discovered the reason stories are so important.

During my high school career, I mostly achieved straight A's, even during the severity of my illness. I was a good student, and just like Rory and Paris, I prided myself on that label. So, I studied the meaning of *The Red Badge of Courage,* analyzed characters like Ralph and Piggy, and memorized *Who's Who and What's What in Shakespeare.* But against this teenage backdrop, my body was falling apart on me. It had taken the Brutus path and betrayed me decades before it was supposed to start deteriorating. Now, my life was pure *Misery* –yet, there I was, writing essays and memorizing facts.

There would be moments when I'd lie in bed surrounded by my books and notes, much like when Rory props up five different textbooks on the kitchen table to read them all at once when she's trying to prepare for finals. In this overwhelmed state, I'd steal a few precious seconds of rest by closing my eyes when I ought to be studying. I'd lie there and think, *What is the point of all this?*

All of the great literature available to us, from *Candide* to *The Master and Margarita,* is inherently missing something. It took over a decade for me to realize that *I* was missing from these stories. You were missing. For some reason, we focus on processing literature without one of the most vital aspects of a book: the reader. For what is a book without a reader?

I know now that literature offers a map when the way ahead seems hazy. In a world where it seems like changes happen every second, stories ground us in universal truths, helping us navigate life's transitions.

In school, we never discussed how these stories affected us, how they challenged us to think, or what they showed us about the world. What if we had been taught to use these stories as a mirror to reflect the truths of our lives so we can see them clearly, such as how *The Art of War* can reveal strategies on how to get through life's battles? What if we interpreted everything–from books like *The Awakening* or *The Razor's Edge* to shows like *Gilmore Girls*–as myths to help us out on our own journeys?

Myths have existed from the beginning of civilization, spanning different cultures and generations, defining our world with their lessons. They relate the experience of being alive by guiding us through adolescence and fostering the transition into adulthood, like in *To Kill a Mockingbird*. They help us endure and process pain and grief, like in *The Crucible*. Myths are emotional, spiritual, and psychological histories of the world that aid us in living. According to Campbell, each hero, no matter whether they are at the bottom of Mount Kilimanjaro, through the wardrobe to Narnia, or in the world we call our own, essentially follows the same pathway called the hero's journey, as outlined in the following stages.

The Call: The hero must leave their point of homeostasis, the current baseline to which "normal life" is attributed.

Supernatural Aid: Advisors with mystical powers (think the gods helping out Odysseus in *The Iliad*) or wise words to aid the hero (as in *The Count of Monte Cristo*).

Obstacles: As a person living on this earth, I'm sure you understand obstacles.

The Belly of the Whale: Think of one of the worst moments in your life, when you thought all was lost and there was no way to escape; that's the belly of the whale.

Moments before Death: A hero's journey always includes a moment of death. (One does not have to die physically.) Like TJ's realization that a lap is an illusion, death is a metaphor.

Death: The old you is gone, never to return; it's essentially dead.

Rebirth: Where there is death, there is also life, a rebirth that always follows. "The Prodigal Daughter Returns," a little sadder but much wiser.

You're a Hero: What was once random and inexplicable now has a purpose because it brought you to this moment in time, to this person you are now.

The Hero's Duty/Return: You must now return to the world you once belonged to and share your newfound knowledge and powers with others.

However, the hero's journey is also cyclical–the process will happen again and again and again.

For years, I've observed characters repeatedly going through this cycle, each journey giving me something new to consider and take with me. Delving into the lessons of *Gilmore Girls* and Campbell's book, also mentioned by Professor Bell in season five, taught me the importance of stories and the tales written and rewritten in each of us. My struggles with chronic illness or with writing were no longer a random act of God; it was a hero's journey, a gauntlet that I had already bested but one I will also face every day of my life.

That doesn't make my path any simpler to walk or my illness less painful to bear. Having something to fight for doesn't make any future trials or trauma less painful, but it does give me something to hold on to. It gives me purpose. If you've ever seen a superhero movie, you know that purpose is power. The feelings I had to face, the lessons I had to learn, and the knowledge I attained are now all a part of the tool kit I use to provide others with the comfort, joy, growth, and transformation that I've found in the written word.

I already had passion and plans that would impress even Paris Geller behind every single one of my dreams, but now they also have meaning. More importantly, I now see how much each of those creations can affect others and how my purpose is to help readers transform their own lives using literature.

Many of you have already undergone such a roller coaster of an adventure for yourself and now recognize the hero's path in your own life, but if you haven't, know that it lies ahead and that you can conquer it. It doesn't matter whether your shared wisdom manifests as a movie, mathematics, or space travel; it will reveal the transformations of your hero's journey and serve as your contribution to the world.

Finding your purpose is no small feat. Some of you may have always known your purpose, just like Luke has always embraced his destiny of helping to care for his community by doing little acts of kindness, such as assisting Mrs. Cassini in crossing the street. However, many others have gone through years of their life feeling as lost as Jess Mariano. But don't worry, life can be like cheese or wine; it gets better with age. So, if you're still searching for that thing that makes you want to get out of bed every morning, here are a few tips to help you.

Tip #1: Kangaroo Like Kirk.

This Stars Hollow townie has practically a million jobs, hopping from one vocation to the next in each episode. Though we don't exactly know why he changes occupations so often, I like to think he's just searching for his passion. By trying out so many different options, Kirk can figure out what resonates with him and what doesn't. So, don't be too scared to change jobs, change industries, or even volunteer; you may find something you love.

After I left my full-time job in sales, I embarked on a journey not only to make money but also to enjoy new experiences. I did some background work on local TV sets (which was super fascinating, by the way), dabbled in freelance writing, and did some consulting in marketing. Writing a book was still the goal, but working in these other areas taught me valuable lessons I could utilize in my future endeavors.

Tip #2: Play Like Paris.

Set up your glue gun and art supplies, and try out any hobby that piques your interest. Sometimes hobbies are just for fun, and that's wonderful, but sometimes they inspire you to start a new venture. I would have never zeroed in on my purpose of helping readers transform their lives if I hadn't been reading Rory's books and watching *Gilmore Girls* just for funsies. So experiment, have fun, travel, be silly and playful, get out of your comfort zone, and get crafty. You never know when inspiration will strike!

Also, look at your favorite books, movies, or TV shows and compare them with the hero's journey. Have you been through any similar experiences that have allowed you to grow? What can you share with others? Contemplate your personal history and lessons learned and see whether that helps narrow down some ideas on your aspirations.

Tip #3: Expand Your Definition of "Juice."

I had to say "juice" because that's how Kirk explains his decision to break his juice diet, but I really mean expanding your definition of purpose. Let's say you want to help people; that could mean many different things. Don't be discouraged if being a nurse isn't your calling; you can still help people by working at the library, painting artwork that inspires people, becoming a teacher, running for a political office, or growing hybrid fruits like rasquats—this list could go on forever, people! Personally, I want to transform lives by writing books, but in the future, I could still do the same by writing a musical. These jobs all feed the same goal; they're just different incarnations of that purpose, so don't be afraid to think outside the box. Feel free to adjust your purpose however it manifests. We all change and grow over the years, so your purpose can too.

Tip #4: We Will Follow.

This one is more of a reminder. An inherent principle of the hero's journey is that all of the universe's previous heroes are there to support the next generation. This means you're not alone in your journey! When things get tough, I find it comforting to remember that we have a whole host of heroes at our backs.

The list of fictional heroes is never-ending, from Becky Sharp from *Vanity Fair* and Eliza from *Uncle Tom's Cabin* to Lemuel Gulliver from *Gulliver's Travels.* Every main character of every movie you've watched and every book you've read has lived through the hero's journey so that you could have someone to be with you on a journey of your own. That's right, Lorelai and Rory, Richard and Emily, Sookie and Jackson, Paris, Lane, and me—we're all here with you, fighting beside you and cheering you on.

And when you are reborn, you will join me and "the chorus of centuries" of heroes imparting their wisdom to the next generation. Our purpose will change the world, one hero, one book, and one TV show at a time.

You're a hero, Gilmore.

And now, for your entertainment, here is a list of actors who have "Kangarooed Like Kirk" and appeared in other Amy Sherman-Palladino series in addition to *Gilmore Girls*.

Bunheads **(2012–2013)**

Picture a young Miss Patty–type Vegas showgirl who marries her admirer and moves to a small Stars Hollow–reminiscent town where she teaches dance to the young ladies. And voilà, you have *Bunheads*.

- Kelly Bishop as Fanny Flowers, the dance teacher
- Rose Abdoo as Sam, the townie who works at Sparkles clothing store
- Liza Weil as Milly Stone, Sparkles landlord and sister to Sparkles owner, Truly
- Sean Gunn as Sebastian, the award-winning coffee barista
- Alex Borstein as "Hooker" Neighbor
- Todd Lowe as Davis, the one-eyed plumber
- Biff Yeager as Bob, Paradise Hardware store worker
- Gregg Henry as Rico, owner of the Oyster Bar
- Chris Eigeman as Conor, a director
- Jon Polito as Sal Russano, owner of Sal's Dancy Pants (dance-wear store)
- Sam Philips also wrote the score

The Marvelous Mrs. Maisel **(2017–2023)**

Remember when Rory and Dean fight about *The Donna Reed Show*? 🎬 Well, picture Donna Reed, then subtract the husband and add a burgeoning career in stand-up comedy in New York, and you basically have the plot of *The Marvelous Mrs. Maisel*.

- Alex Borstein as Susie Myerson, Mrs. Maisel's manager and friend
- Jane Lynch as Sophie Lennon, a comedian
- Emily Bergl as Tessie, Susie's sister
- Kelly Bishop as Benedetta, the matchmaker
- Liza Weil as Carole Keen, the bassist
- Milo Ventimiglia as Sylvio, who has a tryst with Mrs. Maisel
- Sean Gunn as Stewart Jones, "The Roast Master," for Susie's comedic roast event
- Danny Strong as Aaron Lebowitz, an entertainment manager

- Scott Cohen as Solomon Melamid, the *Village Voice* editor
- Chris Eigeman as Gabe, who works with Mrs. Maisel's father

Étoile (2025–)

Yay—another ASP dance-inspired show! There's not much info about this show at the time I'm writing this, but we do know it's about two famous dance companies and their struggle to save their institutions from becoming a thing of the past.

- Yanic Truesdale as Raphael
- Dakin Matthews as Harlan
- Kelly Bishop as Clara

(According to IMDb, the series is already planning its season two, so more of the *Gilmore* family might make an appearance!)

A Complete List of Kirk's Many Jobs

Kirk claims to have worked more than fifteen thousand jobs, and I think we can believe him. For Kirk, no task is too big or too small—or too weird. Here are a few of my favorite "Kirk Careers":

Dragonfly Inn

Custom Mailbox Entrepreneur (Sn 4 Ep 6)
Wood Delivery Guy (Sn 4 Ep 22)
Dragonfly Kitchen Assistant (Sn 5 Ep 12)
Dragonfly Receptionist (Sn 5 Ep 12)
Stars Hollow Board of Tourism Info Map Person (Sn 6 Ep 6)
Real Estate Agent (Sn 6 Ep 17)

Independence Inn

Swan Delivery (Sn 1 Ep 3)
"Hey There" Skincare Founder (Sn 3 Ep 1)
Bracebridge Dinner Server (Sn 2 Ep 10)

Lorelai's House

DSL Installer (Sn 1 Ep 2)

Wedding Photographer (Sn 2 Ep 3)

Mechanic (Sn 2 Ep 7)

Termite Exterminator (Sn 2 Ep 11)

Stars Hollow

Dog Walker (Sn 4 Ep 15)

Wedding DJ (Sn 4 Ep 21)

Political Poll Gatherer (Sn 5 Ep 4)

Dragonfly Lunch Promoter (Sn 5 Ep 6)

Yummy Bartender Proprietor (Sn 6 Ep 9)

Kirk's Diner Proprietor (Sn 7 Ep 2)

Sales Clerk–Stars Hollow Beauty Supply (Sn 3 Ep 12 and Sn 4 Ep 1)

Theater Attendant–Black & White & Read Movie Theater (Sn 5 Ep 14)

Emcee/Announcer–Stars Hollow Hockey Rink (Sn 3 Ep 15)

T-Shirt Entrepreneur (Sn 3 Ep 17)

Mail Boxes Etc. Clerk (Sn 4 Ep 19)

Security Agent–Stars Hollow Security (Sn 4 Ep 4)

You'll Always Have Paris

Getting Out of Our Own Way

"But now I accept it, because I can't control everything."

—Paris (Sn 4 Ep 2)

When we first meet Paris Geller, she's the alpha dog at Chilton, never letting up on her Machiavellian mission to make perfect grades and blasting her way through any obstacle in her path, including teachers and schoolmates. Achievement is everything to Paris, so much so that Rory jokes that Paris never rests but "periodically makes a whirring noise and then shuts down." Laser focused on her goals and avoiding everything resembling a "distraction," including sleep, Paris will do whatever it takes to get what she wants.

Her introduction to Rory, however, causes subtle changes. Together, Geller and Gilmore make an interesting team, collaborating on everything from Shakespeare school projects to student body politics (Rory acting as the friendly *Rebecca of Sunnybrook Farm* to soften Paris's General Sherman on the warpath attitude as student body president). Only Rory can temper Paris's desire to fire the elderly Chilton librarian and open Paris's mind to listening to the other student officials, like when Rory encourages Paris to consider raising the hemlines of their uniforms to garner goodwill with Francie, the senior class president. But the Parisian adventure doesn't end there. Paris decides to attend Yale University after high school and even pulls some strings so she can room with Rory. From college freshman to editor of the *Yale Daily News*, Paris remains the dictator of her own world.

However, Paris's frenzied focus on every minute detail of her battle plans to take over the world keeps her stuck in a cycle of stress and overachievement and prevents her from stepping back and looking at her entire life to determine what's most important. She's missing the "bigger picture," effectively removing herself from the game of life before she's even started. With that in mind, it's clear we have more to learn from Paris than how to flawlessly wear a power suit.

The Paris philosophy is perfectionism and hustle culture times ten. But Paris Mode isn't all it's cracked up to be; in fact, it could be why her Chilton peers don't want to vote for her to be student body president, why she can't get a date for the school formal, and why her social circle is severely limited. Paris is getting in her own way.

If we brought this hypothesis to Paris herself, she'd do her research and craft her findings into a well-written presentation that could only lead the listener to the undeniable truth that they're getting in their own way. So that's what we're going to do too.

The first pitfall of Paris Mode is exemplified by her earliest interactions with Rory. Initially, Rory is seen as a threat, someone who could stand in the way of Paris's plans to be the best. After seeing the Bangles together in New York with Madeline and Louise, Paris begins to let her guard down and offers to let Rory share the debate time for their school project, a very Paris gesture of friendship. However, when Paris's crush, Tristin, asks Rory out in season one, chaos erupts. Rory refuses Tristin's invite, but Tristin tells Paris that Rory is going to the PJ Harvey concert with him. Paris eventually finds out that Tristin is lying, and even though Rory has done nothing wrong, Paris gives Rory the silent treatment for the rest of the school year. Though Paris frequently hangs out with Madeline and Louise in the series, they don't share the goals, secrets, and feelings that Paris only has in common with Rory. Paris's relentless quest to be the best and her rigid rejection of anyone who reveals that she can sometimes be in the wrong effectively kill the budding friendship she has with Rory, her one true friend.

In season three, Rory and Paris are chosen to give a speech at the Chilton Bicentennial. Instead of reciting the speech they had planned, Paris begins to reflect on why she didn't get into Harvard, closing with the revelation that she can have sex (which she believed was an impossible achievement) but she can't get into Harvard (which she thought was a given), and apparently, only virgins like Rory can get into Harvard.

However, upon further bedridden reflection later that week, Paris admits it probably wasn't her relationship with Jamie that precluded her from admission to Harvard; it was her interview. Paris, in her achievement-focused, pressure-filled, impossible standards mindset, does what all pressured things do when they don't get a release: explode. Paris had the misfortune of being in her Harvard interview when she erupts in a population-control diatribe and yells at the admissions officer. Everything she had worked for her entire life was gone in just a few minutes—but did she learn her lesson?

Fast-forward a few years to Paris's appointment as editor of the *Yale Daily News*, something she had set her sights on during her first days at Yale. However, Paris goes a little overboard in her bid to be an excellent editor in chief, making Miranda Priestly from *The Devil Wears Prada* look tame. Paris makes everyone wear numbered hats so she doesn't have to remember their names, requires a tracking system for her staff, endlessly rewrites everyone's articles, and sets up a personal bunker inside the newsroom. None of this improves the paper; it gets so bad that they print one edition with a big blank space where a photo should be. After a typical Paris tirade, most of the staff quits, and the board votes to revoke her title as editor.

Once again, the Paris theatrics, though enjoyable to watch, undid all of her work. The more relentless she is about a goal, the more she seems to move backward instead of forward. After a roller-coaster ride like that, it's easy to see why Paris copes by acting out in the most Paris of ways: by binging medical soap opera shows and kicking Rory out of their shared apartment. The Chilton speech and *The Devil Wears Prada* moment are perfect examples of how too much hustle can lead to burnout.

If anyone could be accused of going full-on Paris, it would be me. Remember that history project with a moat that Paris made and Rory accidentally trashed? I had a high school project exactly like that, and you bet I got an A. I may not stay home on a Friday night to reread the *Iliad*, but I do stay in reading for fun from time to time. So yeah, I'm a total Paris.

I've been through the same circle of burnout, overcorrection, and missing out that Paris so hilariously and heartbreakingly depicts on *Gilmore Girls*. I've worked a typical nine-to-five job, added several side hustles, and worked through weekends on other projects for so long that the word "burnout" seems inadequate to describe my state. In season one, episode fourteen, Rory shares that she's heard her brain "ping," which Lorelai interprets as a sign that Rory is studying too much. Aside from the comical debate over whether Rory's brain made a "pinging" or "dinking" sound, this conversation is a serious reminder of the ramifications of being overworked. I remember my brain felt so broken down that a "dinking" sound would have felt like an encouraging sign of life. Instead, I had a black hole sloshing around my head, devouring any sign of coherent thought.

Of course, I ended up overcompensating for how depleted and frazzled I had become by being extra rigid in my plan-making and organization, which, *surprisingly*, my coworkers did not love. And to top it all off, I was working so hard that I was losing out on everything else life has to offer. My weekends were for either work or forced recovery time, so, just like Paris, I wasn't hanging out with friends, meeting new people, or having fun experiences. Outside of work, I had no life; it was time for something to change.

Let me step in for a moment and be your Lorelai and say that, friend, if your brain is "pinging" or "dinking," like Rory's was, it's time for some rest, because brain pinging is a sure sign of the beginnings of burnout.

So, what do you do when Paris Mode takes over your life? Based on my research, I've developed a burnout-banishing method that will blow your bow ties off. It's called "Make a Plan to Cut Yourself Some Slack"—or, if you will, the Paris–Lorelai formula. Now, I know that title sounds contradictory, but that's part of the plan. For example, when Paris is having trouble deciding where she wants to attend college, she goes around and around with all the data she's collected and all the opinions of others. However, Lorelai encourages Paris to forget all of that and make her decision solely on where she wants to go. Yes, sometimes the Paris method can help you accomplish your goals, but having a Lorelai around to counterbalance the antics is what makes this plan so brilliant. After all, what is life without having to balance something?

Step 1: Make a Plan.

For some reason, it's so much easier to be flexible, spontaneous, and self-restorative if you plan it out. Our time is valuable, and scheduling all the important things helps protect the time you dedicate to them. Write down rest breaks and workouts in your calendar, schedule time with friends, and set up your phone for automatic do-not-disturb hours. Write out all the small steps for your big goals and plan out those tasks across your week. However you like to plan things, digital calendar or bullet journal, do what works for you, but create a detailed plan for all the different areas of your life (money, relationships, health, career, etc.).

Then, when something unexpected comes up, you're more prepared to handle it. In season two, Lorelai tells Luke, "I can be totally flexible as long as everything is the way I want it." Turns out, Lorelai's quip was right; it's easy to be flexible when there are many options; it's more challenging to be flexible when you have nothing, so set up some structure in your life.

Step 2: Let Go.

Personally, I think this is the more difficult part of the plan, but I'm sure others will excel at it. This is the "What would Lorelai do?" part, though you could substitute "What would Sookie do?" as well; no one knows how to throw out the plan like Sookie!

When I started the *Gilmore Book Club* blog, I had a major plan. The site first went live in 2018, but I worked on it for months and months before that. I meticulously played with layouts and fonts, but no fidgeting with the site compared to the endless perfecting I did with the first few essays I planned to post. I wrestled with which quotes to feature, agonized over word choice, and endlessly tweaked paragraphs. I wanted it to be perfect. This was something I had worked so hard on and dreamed about for so long. I wanted it to be perfect not only for my own satisfaction but also for my (soon-to-be) readers.

Because of my perfectionism, I kept pushing out the date I planned for the site to go live, sure that just a few more tweaks would make it good enough and scared of letting something out into the world that wasn't up to my standards. It got to the point where I was unsure whether I would publish at all. That's when my Lorelai, my mom, stepped in. "If you don't do this," she said, "you will always wonder what could have happened. You will always wonder: *What if*?"

My mom's words reminded me of a scene in *Divine Secrets of the Ya-Ya Sisterhood*, when the main character, Siddalee, dreams of riding an elephant named Lawanda but runs for her life upon seeing the enormity of her endeavor. It was only when her mom steps in to remind her that it was Siddalee's dream to ride the elephant in the first place and her fear was getting in the way that Siddalee comes back and rides Lawanda. It's only with that little push that you get out of your own way and ride the elephant. It's just like Paris's obsession with Harvard. She's so laser focused on getting into the school that she doesn't realize she wants to go to Yale until Lorelai tells her the dream is getting in the way of the dream, because the dream isn't Harvard; it's the life and the education that Paris wants that are important. At some point, you have to let go of what's holding you back so you can move forward.

There is a saying that people aren't afraid of failing; they're scared of success. I've never understood that because failing is excruciating. It's so agonizing that we twist ourselves into Paris-shaped pretzels, trying to be so impeccable, hoping that we'll avoid the pain of mistakes and failure. Maybe I don't look like that on the outside, but I sure can pretzel it up on the inside. Mistakes are inevitable, but they're usually fixable. If things do go wrong, you put on your Lorelai Wedding Planner Disaster List hat and fix the problems one by one, and life goes on. At some point, you have to realize the plan is in the past, and you're in the here and now, so you have to be mindfully present to address the situation at hand. You have to jump in; you have to start.

In the show, Lorelai is adept at jumping in, but in real life, Lauren Graham feels different, especially with writing. Her book *Talking as Fast as I Can* details how she felt overwhelmed by the number of written projects she had due and she couldn't write anything. Hello, perfectionism, *Our Mutual Friend.* Thankfully, a friend of hers mentioned the kitchen timer method, which is kind of a different Pomodoro method in which you work for a set amount of time and write *anything* you want. Lauren used this plan to cut herself some slack, and now she has two fantastic essay collections and a fiction book to add to her résumé.

Lorelai and her real-life self, Lauren Graham, are right: at some point, you must realize that being the most extreme version of yourself and not allowing yourself to slide along the scale of your entire ability is holding you back. It's OK to have big dreams and detailed plans, but don't let fear drive you to overwork and overanalyze because that's when you enter the manic Paris territory. Schedule your goals, be strict about self-care, embrace those who push you to grow, and give yourself a break when you need it.

Because if you get in your way, you are just going to end up kicking your own butt. The last person I want to be in my way is myself, so I am committing to taking the Paris–Lorelai formula to heart. But you do what you want. It is, as Rory points out, your own butt and your own future on the line.

Give yourself a break, Gilmore.

A List of the Very Best Paris Moments

- Paris is an expert at Shakespeare; she can intimidate new classmates with recitations of Shakespeare's sonnets, and Puck from *A Midsummer Night's Dream* makes his way into Paris's last moments with her boyfriend. But none can hold a skeleton head (instead of a candle, get it?) to Paris's performance as Romeo to Rory's Juliet. (Sn 2 Ep 9)
- Five, six, seven, eight! Paris puts theater critics to shame by pulling out as many Broadway and dance-related references as she can to intimidate Brad, who has recently returned to Chilton from spending time on the stage in *Into the Woods.* (Sn 3 Ep 16)
- One of my absolute favorite Paris moments springs from a fight with roommate Janet about her football player boyfriend. In an insult that would make Tolkien proud, Paris complains about the dent in their couch, alleging that "Gandalf the Grey is still falling down it; it was a big hole!" (Sn 4 Ep 5)
- Paris receives a gigantic printing press from her dead professor-boyfriend, Asher–you know, as one does. Of course, the printing press is positioned right on Rory's backpack, making it quite difficult for Rory to get to class. Later, when trying out the printing press, Paris declares that Ben Franklin was out of his mind. Pot, meet kettle. (Sn 5 Ep 4)
- I don't have many complaints about *Gilmore Girls*, but being unable to see Paris belly dancing would definitely be one. Only Paris would have dance classes on her "Operation Graduate from Yale" to-do list, and this scene would have been hilarious to watch. (Sn 7 Ep 14)

Behind the Scenes: Daniel Palladino as the Town Loner

Basically, the town loner is *Much Ado About Nothing* in true Stars Hollow style. Not only does he make a great Boo Radley character (which, as Rory points out, you can never have enough of) but also he promotes much debate, attention, speculation, and hilarity without anyone ever knowing who he is or what he's trying to protest in the town square in season three, episode six.

Thanks to costumer extraordinaire Valerie, we do have confirmation that Daniel Palladino plays the town loner and wears a khaki-colored coat in the scene. Plus, we now have the extremely crucial information that the sign had actual gibberish written on it and was positioned on a small portion of the banner so that it was harder for anyone to see, but if you did have eagle eyes and saw something, it was guaranteed you'd see only gobbledygook. Thank goodness I put on my *Encyclopedia Brown* detective hat to solve this vital mystery and we can all sleep soundly in our beds tonight.

Lessons for Pippi Virgins

The Importance of Staying True to Yourself

"... even more than the actual experience of performing live, the confidence it gives you in every aspect of your life–that's the most amazing thing."

—Brad (Sn 3 Ep 16)

The lessons of *Gilmore* would be incomplete without the concepts of home and community, but one can never be truly at home or part of a community without feeling entirely like oneself. We see this uniqueness included in Rory's reading list with titles like *Eloise* and *Emily the Strange* and in the show on one particular Black & White & Read movie night, during which Lorelai and Rory celebrate the singular quirks of Pippi Longstocking by singing along to Pippi's theme song and labeling Luke a "Pippi virgin" because he's never seen the film before. No place embraces the most extraordinary personalities like Stars Hollow.

One of the reasons fans are so devoted to the show's characters, from the central cast to the townies and Rory's classmates, is because every individual is so uniquely themselves and (minus theater-loving Brad and perhaps Paris) is accepted and embraced for who they are.

Let's start this Pippi party with our main girls, Lorelai and Rory. Lorelai Gilmore is a compilation of singular quirks. We've discussed her quick wit and fascinating pop culture mindset, but there's so much more that makes Lorelai so different from anyone else. She warms her socks in the oven and likes her sheets tucked in on both sides of the bed so she can slip in the middle like a straitjacket. She disapproves of her breakfast ogling her; eggs and pancakes must be separated on the plate. And, my favorite Lorelai tradition: she always takes a walk in the first snow of the season. Because, of course, Lorelai always knows when it will snow; she can smell it in the air. (And yes, I'm team you *can* smell snow.)

Rory's peculiarities, while more organizational, are still exceptionally her own. She absolutely cannot have multicolored school supplies; the regular, basic pens and pencils must match the seriousness of the task. She must arrive unnecessarily early to her first classes of the semester to plan her route and familiarize herself with her surroundings. Rory must also be in a location commensurate with the kind of studying she has to do. There's library studying, locked in her room studying, kitchen table or couch studying, even sitting under a tree studying. It doesn't matter whether it's a major life decision or a school project; Rory needs to do all her studying and preparation her way.

If the Gilmore girls are unique, then the residents of Stars Hollow are downright eccentric. Babette and Morey walk their cat in a wagon, complete with a canopied section where Cinnamon can go if she needs some alone time. Taylor measures the height of everyone's lawn and the distance between community buildings and the edge of their property. And then there's Kirk, the epitome of eccentricity, a cornucopia of kooky.

He wakes up at 5 a.m. to get a specific chair at Luke's and keeps a diary tracking the availability of said chair.

Everyone in Stars Hollow accepts one another's quirks, and perhaps sometimes enjoys a laugh at their expense, but most of the time, everyone welcomes those differences as part of what makes it so enjoyable to live there. Lorelai readily accepts Sookie's explanation of Jackson singing to his persimmons in season two (far better than his dancing with the watermelons), and everyone allows Kirk to do his "Kirk in a box" experiment where he hangs out in a glass box suspended above the town square for a few days in season seven. That's a big reason why fans feel at home in Stars Hollow too; they know they are accepted no matter what.

However, at Chilton, things are very different. Most of its students are the progeny of high achievers who highly value status and looks. Existing outside the mold of this way of life is seen as a threat to success rather than something to be embraced. As we discussed in the previous chapter, students like Paris didn't have the luxury of being accepted for who they are. In this world, Rory, too, is initially an outcast, labeled as a goody-goody from the boonies, just taking up space. And Brad, dear, dear Brad, is a complete pariah, ostracized from any Chilton group for his extreme shyness and, later, for his theater experience. Both Rory and Brad have a choice to make: they can stay and adapt to be more like their classmates, become more comfortable standing out, or leave Chilton and find a community that is more amenable to their personalities.

With Lorelai's help and encouragement, Rory chooses to remain at Chilton and adhere to her own personality, even if it won't win her any friends right away. (Brad exits, stage left.) Through all the times the Chilton kids called Rory "Mary" and taunted her over Emily inviting them all to Rory's birthday party, she remains steadfastly herself–and it pays off. Only Rory, with her one-of-a-kind brain and kind heart, could be the sweet Snow White antidote to Paris's terrifying Mother Gothel personality. This allowed Rory to become part of an unstoppable dynamic duo that would build the academic foundation of accolades that helped Rory achieve valedictorian status at Chilton and her acceptance at

Harvard, Princeton, and Yale universities. Only Rory's open-mindedness could get Paris and Jess, two thoroughly opposite people, to sit down and discuss the merits of the Beatniks, 📖 Hunter S. Thompson, 📖 and Jane Austen, 📖 reminding them that each author has a valid space in the annals of literature. Finally, Rory's ability to get everyone on her side in the last-minute rush to get out the *Yale Daily News* after Paris's meltdown eventually earned her the title of editor in chief. Because Rory embraced her own unique combination of personality traits, experiences, and outlook on life, she could accomplish her goals, rise to the top, make friends, and eventually carve out a community for herself.

In a world that so often equates "different" with "bad," it's easy to assume that Lorelai and Rory would be outcasts, but their individuality is precisely why they are so beloved. They are fresh, new, exciting, and funny, and their charisma immediately draws others in. Popular slogans in the *Gilmore* community, such as "Read like Rory" and "Drink coffee like Lorelai," celebrate this genuine aspect of the show, and honorary Gilmores devote their time to re-creating everything from the character's literature and eating habits to their outfits and surroundings. Fans want to tap into that spirit of self-acceptance and celebrate their own unique qualities, something that we desperately need in today's never-ending parade of prequels, sequels, and reboots. I understand the reassurance and safety of conformity, but there is also comfort in knowing that people love and support you as you are. There can also be excitement and incredible discoveries in forging your own path, and those moments can be the icing on the Pop-Tart of life.

If there's one character scared of branching out, it's Brad Langford, Chilton's resident shy guy. He's always cowering in Paris's tirades and shrinking as far back into the shadows as he can until he leaves Chilton entirely, but even a switch to another school doesn't solve his extreme diffidence. What Brad needs is a little help from Stephen Sondheim via the composer's fairy tale masterpiece *Into the Woods*. Yes, Brad spends some time on Broadway as Jack, the little boy who talks to his cow in the legendary musical. It's this experience that completely changes

Brad. Sometimes, you have to step out of your comfort zone and find a community of people who embrace their own uniqueness in order to finally be comfortable in your own skin.

Like Brad, I, too, found my confidence in the theater. From kindergarten to eighth grade, I continuously struggled to connect with my peers. I sometimes even preferred to talk to adults, feeling that I understood them better and that they understood me. However, everything changed when I earned a spot in the local production of *The Music Man*. 🎬 Suddenly, my artistic inclinations weren't abnormal; they were celebrated and even required for what I was about to do. My world now included lengthy dance rehearsals, learning to flip over my partner's back, and memorizing the steps for entire scenes. When we weren't dancing, we were singing, practicing harmonies and crescendos, and, of course, acting. This group of artists understood me. But more importantly, these people were open to the world and, therefore, open to me. In a way, they were Gilmores.

From the barbershop melodies in *The Music Man* to the Latin prayers in *The Sound of Music*, 🎬 I loved it all. (And yes, I can still sing my second soprano part in Latin as Nun #3 for "Morning Hymn.") The theater taught me that my kind of people were out there and that I didn't have to change who I was to be loved. Even when I was no longer with them, the acceptance I felt within their ranks boosted my confidence in other situations and helped me navigate a world where acceptance isn't always guaranteed.

And that's what happened to Brad too. He returned to Chilton after his stint on Broadway, and though, in essence, he was still the same quirky kid, he was more self-assured and held up better under the peer pressure at school. In an ending only Brad Langford could (or would) do, he sang a portion of his graduation speech at Chilton, confidently belting out, "Cherish is the word I use to describe . . ." Go ahead and sing it out, Brad, because even Walt Whitman had to learn how to say "I celebrate myself." 📖

Being true to yourself is an essential step in having a full life, but as we saw with Rory, it can also help you accomplish your goals. My obsession with *Gilmore Girls* got me my first book deal, so staying true to myself has worked out pretty well for me, but I wasn't always as confident in my quirkiness as I am now.

Just like Brad and me, Amy Sherman-Palladino has also felt the pressure to conform to the ways of others. Amy shared with the 2015 ATX Television Festival audience that she did things differently from many experts in the television industry. Amy wanted to include all this sparkling dialogue, much more than is traditionally allowed, and executives told her it was too much. Of course, when filmed, they ended up with a program that wasn't long enough and had to shoot more. Amy had been right. Then, when they had to play for time, executives wanted to re-create elements, like the *Frasier* animations, that had been done on other shows, but Amy argued that she didn't want to be a copy of another series. Plus, those elements wouldn't be genuine to the feel of *Gilmore Girls* either. (I don't know about you, but I think that any animation would have interrupted the feel of *Gilmore Girls*, and I'm so glad Amy listened to her instincts on that one.) After all of that, look where Amy Sherman-Palladino is now! She's had worldwide success in *Gilmore Girls* and *The Marvelous Mrs. Maisel*—all because she fought for her particular vision and point of view. Sometimes, being different is your superpower.

I've also experienced moments where my unique perspective was dismissed by my peers. In one college film course, I made a short film about a dancer who had a chronic illness but continued to dance. My classmates laughed in my face, trashing the film based on its "unrealistic" story and characters. The teacher condoned the criticism, even though this story, however far-fetched, was my own! I was a dance minor, dancing most days of the week. Though I struggled with so much movement because of my illness, I stuck with it because I simply loved to dance.

I remember raging to my mother over the phone as I described the attack in class that day. "They just don't like anyone who dares to be different," she told me. (How true that is of all societies, not just artists.) Now that I've had some distance, it's easy to see how prejudiced they were to anything and anyone who was *Divergent*.

But our society, especially entertainment industries, is dependent on fresh, new ideas. I mean, the Academy of Motion Pictures has awarded Oscars to movies with elves, dwarves, and magic rings and, more recently, a woman who fell in love with a fish-man! Many of these movies were also based on best-selling books that dared to be different and ended up selling millions of copies, winning numerous awards, and staying integral parts of the literary world for generations. Although these novels weren't for everyone, each of those authors eventually found the audience they deserved, the audience that appreciated the magic of people who are one of a kind.

Pippi Longstocking and the Gilmores make being true to yourself look as easy as getting Luke to pour you another cup of coffee, but we all know that the "journey to genuine" is fraught with obstacle after obstacle. Our world isn't always as accepting as I found the theater actors to be or as Stars Hollow is, but that makes it all the more important to find these pockets of acceptance and carry that feeling out into the world. As the Life and Death Brigade at Yale helps Rory embrace one-in-a-lifetime opportunities, find a group that helps you embrace your true personality.

Away from these inclusive groups, it may not be easy to be the one standing out, like being green in a school full of pink princess Glindas, but don't let that hold you back. Along with many other colorful characters from pop culture, Pippi, Lorelai, Rory, Brad, and Amy have shown us that what sets you apart makes you special and uniquely powerful, and you deserve to be celebrated and loved for who you are.

You do you, Gilmore.

The Gilmores' Best of Broadway

No one can reference Broadway like the Gilmores (and Paris)!

The Lion King

"We had no idea we were walking into *The Lion King* without the puppet heads."

—Lorelai (Sn 2 Ep 6)

The Music Man

"When standards slip, families flee and in comes the seedy crowd. You got trouble, my friends."

—Taylor

"Right here in River City!"

—Lorelai (Sn 1 Ep 14)

West Side Story

"I really was just dropping off some food, so don't get all *West Side Story* on me, OK?"

—Jess (Sn 2 Ep 16)

Into the Woods

"Into the woods at Grandma's house . . ."

—Paris (Sn 3 Ep 16)

The Sound of Music

"Somewhere in my youth or childhood . . ."

—Lorelai

"You must have done something good."

—Chris (Sn 7 Ep 4)

South Pacific

"'You've been my inspiration, my rock, my light. I loved you in *South Pacific.*' Hey, when did you do *South Pacific*?"

—Lorelai (reading Rory's yearbook) (Sn 3 Ep 21)

The Producers

"Think how easy *Producers* tickets would be to get."

—Lorelai (if Lorelai married Matthew Broderick) (Sn 2 Ep 14)

Deleted Scene Summary: Season 7, Episode 5, "The Great Stink"

Stars Hollow is suffering from the profusion of pickles, causing an unimaginable stench across the entire town. April puts her *The New Way Things Work* brain to the task and comes to the rescue, once again proving that being a bit different can be good! She explains to Stars Hollow the science of why you light a match in the bathroom, you know, to get rid of smells. Then, she and Luke build a giant bonfire in the town square to combat the odor of the pickles. The whole town gathers around the fire, roasting marshmallows and Kirk's banana boat. Though Taylor is upset that the bonfire is breaking town ordinances, the residents intimidate Taylor into giving in, and they all spend a lovely Stars Hollow evening around the fire.

Let's Be Friends When We're Dead

Preserving the Connections That Sustain Us

Sookie: "Think we'll still be friends when we're dead?"
Lorelai: "I will if you will."

—(Sn 3 Ep 20)

As much as we love *Gilmore Girls*' romantic relationships, the show's friendships are the true love story. From the pilot episode to the finale, the strength of these bonds holds the show together, wrapping the viewer in the feelings of support and love that only the best of friends can offer.

Let's start the friendship festivities with Sookie and Lorelai. The two met while working at the Independence Inn and have been best friends ever since. From double-dating and concerts to everyday activities like errands and going to work, the duo does it all with punny pizazz and heartfelt sentiments. As much as I enjoy their dessert sushi–making shenanigans, their displays of loyalty are what I admire most. Sookie St. James, chef at the Independence Inn and later Lorelai's partner at the Dragonfly, is the definition of loyalty. In the pilot episode, she offers to sell anything she owns to help Lorelai put Rory through Chilton. A few episodes later, Sookie's making late-night Häagen-Dazs Chocolate Chocolate Chip milkshakes for Lorelai and Rory because they're staying at her home to avoid the termites eating theirs. Sookie even stays up all night baking pies so Stars Hollow can give Rory a worthy Bon Voyage party in season seven. Now, that's what I call the Perks of Having a Loyal Best Friend.

Side note—all of these steadfast examples are how I knew there was only one person to use as the muse for naming my first cane. Yes, I name inanimate objects, just like Lorelai named the toaster "Poppy." There's a lot of stigma and shame surrounding accessibility tools like canes and wheelchairs, and I had internalized those feelings for years. So, when I finally began working through those emotions and decided to buy a cane, I named it after Sookie so that whenever I picked it up, I'd automatically have a devoted and supportive friend by my side.

Lorelai, on the other hand, doesn't always reciprocate this unwavering loyalty. There are times when Lorelai is in emotional upheaval and lashes out at Sookie. For example, when Lorelai is scared of how attached she's getting to Max in season one, she initially puts down Sookie's love life instead of addressing her own. Still, she holds up her end of the friendship with acts of devotion by attending Sookie's at-home birth and then later babysitting Sookie's kids on her day off. Yes, readers, a friendship must go both ways!

Then we have Rory and Lane, who met on their first day of kindergarten, and the rest is BFF history. There's something so comforting about a friend you've known forever; there's an understanding, a cozy nostalgia that permeates the relationship, making it feel easy and relaxing. This is Rory and Lane. They hang out and do their homework together, listening to music and talking about boys and even finding creative ways to communicate when Lane is grounded. When Mrs. Kim kicks Lane out of their house, Lane's first instinct is to turn to Rory, bunking in her Yale dorm until Lane figures out her next step. Before Rory leaves Stars Hollow in the final season, she and Lane sit on the front porch, reminiscing about first kisses and how they've always felt like sisters in addition to being friends. This sweet moment signifies Lane as a "home away from home" for Rory to always remember.

Rory's relationship with Paris is quite different from that with Lane, but that's part of what makes it so memorable. Initially rivals at Chilton, Rory and Paris took the long road to friendship, with each intellectual discussion and cultural debate bringing them closer over the years. They even end up as roommates for most of their time at Yale. Though these Chilton alums are not immune to driving each other crazy, they're also a team that pushes the other to be better, or as Paris puts it, a "pace car or Björn Borg." Rory is always on hand to help Paris brainstorm ways to improve the newspaper and provide financial guidance when Paris's family loses all their money in season six. For her part, Paris Geller is fiercely loyal, even yelling at Lucy about how great a friend Rory is and berating Logan for how he treats Rory. And, my personal favorite, Paris hides books in the store so that Rory can buy them later and not have to deal with someone else's notes already in the margins. Now that's friendship! While it's essential that a friend meet you where you are, they must also recognize and accept the person you are growing to be. All of us will change over the years, so your friendships have to evolve with you too.

While the previously named BFFs are primarily in the limelight on the show, I also want to mention my favorite townies: Miss Patty and Babette. These two are an absolute hoot, whether they're squishing around on Luke's diner chairs because they think they're different or distracting town meetings by suggesting Patty play a beat on the bongos. They also make a great team, showing off their singing chops by harmonizing the national anthem for the Stars Hollow hockey game and putting on their own show at karaoke night. There are so many ways to be a friend, but Patty and Babette are proof that if you're not having at least a little fun, you're not doing it right.

Unlike Rory, who has had the same best friend since kindergarten, I've experienced lots of stress over the years in this area. In elementary school, every time I made a new friend, they'd move away and I'd have to

start over! However, I'm lucky to have finally found a person who is Sookie and Lane all rolled into one: my best friend, Andrea. We met my sophomore year in high school bonding over our mutual aversion to *High School Musical*, then at the height of its popularity. We soon became inseparable, living in the same neighborhood, taking the same classes, working at the same gift shop, participating in local theater productions, and singing together in choir. At one point, our choir teacher informed us that our voices did not blend well and we shouldn't sit together, but we completely ignored that and sat next to each other every day for two years—a total Patty and Babette move if ever there was one.

Andrea and I can talk about everything and nothing, sing at the top of our lungs, or sit in an easy silence. Sometimes, the mark of true friendship is knowing you can tell someone anything, such as when Rory told Lane about having an affair with Dean. I knew Andrea was my forever friend the night we drove home from theater practice in complete silence. It had been a long day of rehearsal, and we were tired. We could have remarked on what homework we still had to complete or who was crushing on whom in the cast, but with our fatigue, words took too much energy. Instead, in the quiet moments of the evening, our hearts silently shared a miraculous exchange that only a lifelong bond could yield.

But just as Lane and Rory had to rediscover what their friendship would be like after

Lane married Zack, Andrea and I also had to navigate a change in our relationship. Andrea was marrying a wonderful man, and I couldn't have been happier. I had been there to help pick out her dress, to toast her at her bachelorette party, and finally, to walk down the aisle as her maid of honor. As thrilled as I was to support them in their love story, I had a significant sense of Emma Woodhouse déjà vu. It's surreal to stand beside your best friend as they pledge their life to someone else, to knowingly give up a relationship that's exclusively yours, to willingly step aside and let someone else share the closeness, even overshadow the closeness of you and your best friend in the entire world, but that's exactly what I was doing.

I wonder whether Lorelai felt this way before marrying Max, thinking she'd have to give up a part of her friendship with Rory to be a good wife. Lorelai tells Rory it will no longer be the "me and you secret special clubhouse no boys allowed thing" once Max is in the picture (Sn 2 Ep 3). It's understandably scary to think of losing what made a relationship so extraordinary. With all the flutter of activity that comes with a wedding, I hadn't really thought about this until months after Andrea's nuptials. Would her marriage change everything about our friendship?

But as Rory realistically and somewhat sleepily points out (because her conversation with Lorelai takes place in the middle of the night), she and Lorelai are not dying or going anywhere. Plus, they won't be attacked by giant man-eating ants (gross!), and Lorelai needs to adjust, like when she had green streaks in her hair. All this insect and cosmological commentary really means that *nothing* is changing. Rory and Lorelai make the relationship magical, not the people they're surrounded by. As long as the two of them still dedicate the same love, support, and loyalty to each other, their relationship will stay intact and grow into something that's possibly more wonderful than it was before.

With that in mind, I was determined to adopt a different outlook on my relationship with Andrea. That summer after the wedding, she visited me in New York for a few days. Even though she was one of my favorite people in the world, I was scared something had irrevocably changed between us and we wouldn't be able to connect like we used to. As soon as she arrived, we fell back into our easy comradery as if no time or distance had passed. That week, I began to see that even though our circumstances may have changed, just like Lane and Rory, our friendship was still the same.

Of course, situations will arise, such as when Rory becomes super wrapped up in her relationship with Dean back in season two and Lane, feeling abandoned, decides to become a cheerleader. Despite it all, Rory and Lane are still BFFs, bonding over coffee and listening to their favorite music. Their reconciliation doesn't happen magically; however, they both have to make an effort to come together, apologize for their mistakes, and work it out. Andrea and I may not be debating becoming cheerleaders, but we still have to negotiate the trials life throws at us. We must be committed to adjusting when necessary. Sometimes, friends must bend, but just because we bend doesn't mean we'll break.

Andrea may be someone's wife now, but that doesn't alter the foundations of our friendship. I know she is still mine, my best friend, my family. Because of my relationship with her, I've realized how blessed we are to retain such a strong connection despite the distance and time spent apart; it's a rare gift I'll always cherish. Andrea and I have known each other for over a decade, and I know our friendship will survive and flourish for decades more. And I can confidently say that she and I will still be friends when we're dead.

So when you find that person, don't just hold on tight; invest in growing with them and adapting to whatever life brings your way. Build a strong foundation of friendship; just maybe use something sturdier than Rory's pink-feather-boa hammer, because although friendship is fun, it also takes effort. Sometimes, friends come in and out of our lives for different reasons, and that's OK. But when you find the Sookie to your Lorelai, the Lane to your Rory, or the Miss Patty to your Babette, cherish that friendship and do everything to ensure you're both in it for the long haul.

Let's always be friends, Gilmore.

Top Gilmore BFF Moments

There are just too many fantastic BFF moments to fit in one essay! So here are some additional scenes that show why *Gilmore* besties are so endearing.

Season 1

- Episode 12: Sookie and Jackson are finally going on their first date, but Jackson's surly cousin Rune is in town and threatens to put the kibosh on the entire evening. However, Lorelai agrees to be Rune's date, much to his disappointment, and though Lorelai isn't having any fun, Jackson and Sookie end up having a lovely first date.
- Episode 13: Rory invites Madeline, Louise, and Paris to the Bangles concert in New York. As they jam to "Walk Like an Egyptian," Paris and Rory begin to bond over their reaction to Madeline and Louise's antics, marking the beginning of Rory and Paris's friendship.

Season 2

- Episode 2: Sookie plans an over-the-top wedding shower for Lorelai and Max, complete with heart-shaped pastries with "Max and Lorelai" written on them, ice sculptures, four cakes, and every pink confection imaginable.
- Episode 16: Rory has the house to herself, but Paris makes a surprise visit to strong-arm Rory to help her study. Jess brings over food, and he, Paris, and Rory have a lively debate about Jack Kerouac, Charles Bukowski, and Jane Austen over burgers and fries. But when Dean comes over, finds Jess, and becomes upset, Paris intervenes, telling Dean that she has a crush on Jess and that Rory was only trying to help Paris spend more time with Jess. Paris may not get Jack Kerouac, but she does understand Girl Code.

Season 3

- Episode 1: Rory helps Paris get ready for her date with Jamie. Rory even allows Paris to shut her in the closet so that Jamie doesn't see Rory looking "dateable" and want to go out with her instead of Paris.
- Episode 4: In an act of rebellion against Mrs. Kim's rules, Lane decides to dye her hair purple. So, Rory dutifully applies the bleach and purple dye. However, Lane freaks out in anticipation of Mrs. Kim's reactions, so she makes Rory sneak out of the house, run back to the beauty supply shop, buy black hair dye, sneak back in, and dye Lane's hair back to black.

Season 4

- Episode 3: Sookie is excited to team up with Lorelai to cater a *Lord of the Rings* 🎬 birthday party, but Sookie's idea of what kids want is *very* different from what they actually want. When she accidentally makes a little girl cry, Sookie panics about being a bad mother to her own children. However, Lorelai makes her feel better by telling Sookie she'll be a good mom because Sookie was so good with Rory.
- Episode 18: A.k.a. the year Stars Hollow doesn't make an egg map. Gypsy and Jackson join the group helping to locate the remaining eggs still hidden from the Easter egg hunt a few weeks prior. The pair has a hilarious time making jokes about Taylor's toupee, getting along so well that I wish we had more Gypsy and Jackson moments to make us smile.

Season 5

- Episode 12: The Dragonfly isn't haunted; it's just Sookie, secretly sneaking into an unoccupied room so she can snuggle up in bed, eat Toblerones, watch *Dark Shadows*, 🎬 and have a night all to herself. When Jackson is concerned that Sookie is working too much, Lorelai investigates and finds not a ghost but Sookie. After they talk it out, Lorelai joins Sookie for an episode of *Dark Shadows*.

- Episode 18: It's the debut of the Stars Hollow Museum, but Rory, Paris, and Lane are more concerned about their boy problems. Together, they sit outside and air their grievances, giving viewers a taste of just how entertaining this trio can be.

Season 6

- Episode 1: Babette and Miss Patty are at it again! This time, they're questioning Luke about his recent engagement to Lorelai, but somehow, it turns into a story about how Morey proposed to Babette during a game of Twister.
- Episode 14: Michel shows he cares in the most confusing ways. He starts off by yelling at Luke about his repairs at the inn, then gets into an argument with Lorelai about the previous argument with Luke. However, Michel finally admits that he's upset because he and Lorelai always used to go to Weston's Bakery to make a list for the handyman, which they haven't done since Luke started to fix things, and Michel misses those coffee and cake dates with Lorelai.

Season 7

- Episode 2: When Rory is having trouble connecting with Logan while he's in London and Lane is freaking out because she's pregnant, they both hang out in the bookstore researching their respective issues (*Sexus* 📖 for Rory and *What to Expect When You're Expecting* 📖 for Lane). While they do find some helpful information in books, it's the comfort and advice they give each other that really makes a difference.
- Episode 12: Paris to the rescue! When Rory has a misunderstanding with a new friend, Lucy, Paris comes to Rory's defense. Sure, Paris also wants Rory to concentrate on their conversation about graduation plans, but the loyalty is still what counts. Paris tells Lucy that "anyone should feel lucky to call [Rory] a friend," and the path toward reconciliation is set in motion.

Profiles of Best-Friend Pairs in a Supporting Role

Let's take a moment to recognize these ancillary best-friend duos that will always have a special place in our hearts.

Lucy and Olivia

Or the "Girls Gone Wild" friends, as Paris calls them. Lucy and Olivia are fellow Yale students who meet Rory in their senior year. Olivia is an artist, and Lucy is studying acting. Open to new friends and new experiences, these two are up for anything, from making Rice Krispie treats or expensive popcorn to planning the hairstyles and outfits for their Swedish rock band, the Forbidden Fjords.

Madeline and Louise

Though they're also friends with Paris, Madeline and Louise have a dynamic that is all their own. They're totally in sync regarding the intricacies of lipstick shades and how to be the queens of spring break. Yes, these two know how to party, but they also know how to stay together, even when they attend separate colleges.

Colin and Finn

Ah yes, our Life and Death Brigade bad boys, Colin and Finn. As riotous as they are together, they also have their distinct personalities: Colin is a little aloof and above it all, even maintaining a distance from the milkmaid who followed him home from Holland. Finn is more rambunctious, always making a pass at Rosemary, reenacting the *Passion of the Christ* 🎬 to cheer Rory up, and going through naked phases.

A Yen for Fez

How Traveling Can Manifest Inspiration and Creativity

Richard: "I suspect you have a yen for travel."
Rory: "I'm up to my ears in yens."

—(Sn 1 Ep 3)

Have you ever been forced into something that, to your surprise, you end up liking, maybe even loving? Rory and Richard Gilmore certainly have. In season one, episode three, when Emily declares that Richard should take Rory to their club for a round of golf to help fulfill her Chilton physical education requirement, no one is thrilled. After some awkwardness and some divot-producing golfing on Rory's part, Rory and Richard take a walk under the tree-lined pathway on the club's grounds. It's this walk that changes everything. Rory is soon regaling Richard with the list of cities on her travel bucket list. This conversation between grandfather and granddaughter, this wanderlust, is the seed that allows their relationship to bloom.

In the show's first season, Rory quickly relates Lorelai's regret that she hadn't had the chance to travel more when she was young and establishes her own desire to travel. Through Rory's books, she's roamed all over the world, but she's seen these faraway places only in her mind's eye and the pages of a book, never in real life. Now that she's read about these locations, she wants to experience them for herself and, as she tells Headmaster Charleston, include her adventures in her future career.

Lorelai, however, has curated a desire to see the world because of her natural curiosity, her innate sense of adventure, and the prodigious inclusion of travel in her parents' lifestyle. She was used to Emily and Richard regularly planning luxurious, extended trips to foreign destinations. In fact, they later announced at a Friday Night Dinner that they always go to Europe every two years, always in the fall. Sounds nice, right?

No matter *why* they planned their travel bucket list, Rory and Lorelai both have a desire to see what lies outside the humble town of Stars Hollow. So, they plan the ultimate backpacking trip to celebrate Rory's graduation from Chilton. It includes several months of wandering through Europe, sleeping in hostels, and riding the train. Some aspects may not sound as glamorous or luxurious as Emily and Richard would require, but it's still the trip of Rory's dreams. While we aren't privy to Lorelai and Rory's antics across the pond, we do catch a few anecdotes once they've returned home: Lorelai touched the pope's car in Rome, they waited for Bono in Ireland, and they found a store in Copenhagen where they bought Richard's Queen of Hearts pipe.

If Rory's first European excursion was about sightseeing on a budget, her second was about traveling in luxury. The beginning of season five shows Rory and Emily arriving in Rome, shopping till they drop, and, of course, never moving their own luggage. Emily even has "European luggage," which implies that she has a different set of bags for domestic journeys and international voyages; heaven forbid you use the same suitcase for everything! As much as I'm sure Richard and Emily relish their spectacular trips, I believe a part of this enjoyment stems from their view of travel as an aspect of status. We know Richard's mother, Trix, traipsed all over Egypt to view the pyramids and was once stranded in Istanbul, so we can conclude that she raised Richard on the importance and benefits of exploring the world.

And just what are those benefits? It took the experience of a lifetime and a trip back to the last place on my travel bucket list for me to find out.

It may seem odd, but France was never high in the rankings of places I wanted to visit. My bucket list included bookish sites in England and historical locations in Italy and Greece, but besides the famed Hall of Mirrors in the Palace of Versailles, there wasn't much I wanted to see in France. When I was in college, one of my friends was studying abroad in Leeds, England, and my friends and I planned to meet up with her in London and spend several days there. Initially, we discussed taking a train from there to Edinburgh, but my friends wanted to add a few days in Paris to our itinerary instead. So, I put all research on Scotland aside and dove into Paris travel guides. I planned for us to see it all, and we did: the Louvre, the Eiffel Tower, a walk down the Champs-Élysées, Notre-Dame, and the Palace of Versailles. We had seen what felt like all of Paris. I had thought it would feel romantic and glamorous, like *Funny Face*, 🎬 but to me, the City of Lights lacked the radiance I had expected. So, as type-A list-makers like Rory and Paris love to do, I checked France off my wish list, and that was that.

As fate would have it, the door to France opened once again. At the time, I still worked in the lingerie industry, and I was scheduled to attend the annual International Lingerie Show that's held in Paris in January. A few months later, I was on an airplane, heading to the city I thought I'd never see again. This time, I was determined to change my outlook. This time, Victor Hugo, his famous novel (*The Hunchback of Notre Dame* 📖), and a host of Rory's favorite writers would be coming with me to Paris to show me the way.

Over the preceding months, I had felt the light in my soul grow so dim and feeble that a strong gust of wind would have extinguished it. As the days stretched on seemingly without end, my soul weathered life's blizzards and tornados, starved for inspiration and the restorative waters of fulfilling one's dreams. Nevertheless, I trudged on.

Being an artist can feel like you're spending your life chasing the spark of inspiration that will take you to your next great idea. All too often, that glow is elusive, rare, and fleeting, but when you find it, when that spark hits your heart, there's an overwhelming sense of excitement and purpose, a bright light to wipe out the dust and shadows that have tormented your soul for far too long. Now, I stood before the Notre-Dame Cathedral, gazing up at the intricate facade adorned with saints of stone. As the falling snow muffled the audible traces of the outer world, I began to feel a change on the horizon.

Three hundred and eighty-seven steps, if I remember correctly, separate the streets of Paris from the cathedral's choir of bells and their gargoyle companions. With aching legs, I ascended to the top. The City of Light stretched out before me, the cityscape now a snow globe full of streets, stunning architecture, and iconic monuments. Then, a sound so compelling and pure erupted from behind me. The chime of the bells reverberated around me, and it felt as if Notre-Dame was reminding me to dream again. As the bells rang, I envisioned Quasimodo climbing the steps to his beloved bells, Esmerelda dancing upon her cobblestone stage, and the sinister eyes of Claude Frollo peering at his prey through the darkness. For there I was at the inspirational birthplace for *The Hunchback of Notre Dame*.

Victor Hugo had seen a story behind the stone towers and belfry of the magnificent cathedral. He had heard the peal of the bells and the voices of his characters, whispering their dreams, their agonies, and their grief to him. He wrote and poured his talent, energy, and devotion onto the page, and *Hunchback* was created. Artists wholeheartedly offer themselves upon the altar of creativity, often sacrificing their time and energy to maintain the moment of inspiration and bring their work to life. Who knows how or when the muses will whisper an idea in your ear; like Zack sitting in Luke's with his eyes closed waiting for his muse, you could be waiting awhile, but going out into the world to experience new sounds, textures, cultures, words, architecture, habits, foods, history, and so much more will certainly help. As I stood at the summit of Notre-Dame, such an iconic, literary, and historical place, I heard the melodies of creativity call out to me, and I wanted more.

I strolled down the path to Sainte-Chapelle and stood in awe of the stained-glass windows that seemed to stretch down from the heavens, gracing us mortals with a glimpse of divinity. I browsed through stacks of books in two popular bookshops nearby, reverently running my fingers down the spines of countless novels as if trying to absorb their knowledge with a simple touch. Each new discovery swept my dust-covered soul clean, letting the light of my dreams radiate clearly again, and I felt inspired to rededicate myself to my writing.

I've been incredibly blessed that work has taken me back to Paris a few times since that trip to Notre-Dame, and I intentionally try to discover something new each time. Recently, I've been immersing myself in the details of the Parisian writing culture, delving into the accounts of Ernest Hemingway, Dorothy Parker, and F. Scott Fitzgerald and their time in Paris and all over Europe. While I haven't visited all of the locations their memoirs and biographies have mentioned, I have been able to make a pilgrimage to Shakespeare and Company, where Henry Miller, Allen Ginsberg, and William Styron, in addition to the aforementioned authors, had all gathered once upon a time. With each chance to visit such a place, I feel a connection to the inspirations of the past and a pull toward the future and what my imagination can create.

Sometimes, travel can bring new ideas into focus, allowing you to push past the boundaries that previously held you in place and granting your arrival at a better destination than you could have imagined. Elizabeth Barrett Browning's writing and personal life flourished after moving from London to Italy, and Henry James began his illustrious career by producing travel writing and later finding his niche describing the American experience abroad. And why did their adventures help their literary careers? Travel is said to "increase both cognitive flexibility and depth and integrativeness of thought," according to Adam Galinsky, a social psychologist. Traveling can literally change, even improve, the way you think.

While traveling abroad is an incredible experience, you don't have to journey across an ocean to access the benefits of exploration.

All you need to do is get out of your comfort zone. That could mean exploring a different district in your own city, taking a quick day trip to another area, or visiting a neighboring state or country. Our world is full of incredible places to see and beautiful vistas to admire—all equally worth investigating and capable of providing that spark of inspiration.

So, take every travel adventure possible and be inspired and reenergized by it like a Gilmore. Experience everything you can: watch films, read books, listen to music, travel the world, and never stop learning. Value ancient ruins as much as modern-day attractions, and seek out international destinations as much as locations in your own neighborhood. Keep your soul open to the world, for you never know where your next inspiration awaits you.

Bon Voyage, Gilmore!

Character Recs for Your Next European Trip

All aboard! We're about to travel the world like a Gilmore. Consider this your personalized Gilmore travel guide, pointing you to the best, and the Gilmore-iest, places all over the world. Each destination and attraction has been carefully chosen, either a direct reference from the show or a reflection of the locations I think the Gilmores would love. (And maybe it will inspire you for your next Asian or South American trip too!)

Paris, France

- Shakespeare and Company Bookstore* –Rory and Paris

* Not explicitly mentioned in the show, but the character would love and recommend.
When the book icon appears in the section title, all books listed are from the Rory Gilmore Reading Challenge.

- Notre-Dame Cathedral –Rory
- Jim Morrison's Grave –Rory and Lane
- Monet's Garden –Lorelai
- Tea at the Ritz –Emily
- Eiffel Tower –Emily

London, England

- The Globe Theatre and the George Inn Pub* –Rory and Paris
- Foyles Bookstore, Daunt Books Bookstore* –Rory and Paris
- Hampstead Heath Walk* –Rory and Paris
- Oxford Day Trip –Paris
- Harrods Department Store* –Emily
- The Grapes Pub* –Lorelai and Rory
- Masterclass at the Tea House* –Sookie
- Piccadilly Circus –Logan

Athens, Greece

- National Archaeological Museum –Richard and Rory
- The Acropolis: The Parthenon, the Theatre of Dionysus, and the Temple of Athena –Richard and Rory
- Shopping in Plaka* –Emily
- Shopping in Monastiraki* –Lorelai

The Netherlands

- Anne Frank House –Sookie, Paris, Rory
- The Hague* –Rory and Paris
- Leiden and the Tulip Fields* –Lorelai
- Zaanse Schans and Windmills –Lorelai

Ireland

- Trinity College Library* (Dublin) –Rory
- Oscar Wilde House (Dublin) –Rory
- James Joyce Center (Dublin) –Rory

- The Clarence Hotel (Dublin) –Lorelai
- C. S. Lewis Trail (Belfast) –Rory

Portugal

- Livraria Lello & Irmão* (Porto) –Rory and Paris

Travel Locally Like a Gilmore

Washington, DC

- Folger Shakespeare Library* –Paris
- Smithsonian Natural Museum of American History (Archie Bunker's Chair) –Rory
- Ted's Bulletin's Pop-Tarts* –Lorelai
- Daughters of the American Revolution Museum* –Emily
- Mint Juleps at Round Robin Bar* –Richard

Connecticut

- Mark Twain House & Museum and Harriet Beecher Stowe Center (Hartford) –Rory
- Yale University Library (New Haven) –Rory
- New England Carousel Museum* (Bristol) –Lorelai
- Mayflower Inn and Spa* (Washington) –Lorelai and Emily

Illinois

- American Writers Museum* (Chicago) –Rory
- Ernest Hemingway's Birthplace (Oak Park) –Rory
- Frank Lloyd Wright Home and Studio (Oak Park) –Lorelai
- The Rookery Building (Chicago) –Rory

* Not explicitly mentioned in the show, but the character would love and recommend.
When the book icon appears in the section title, all books listed are from the Rory Gilmore Reading Challenge.

Massachusetts

- Harvard University (Boston) –Rory
- Emily Dickinson's Home (Amherst) –Rory
- Emerson House, Alcott House, Walden Pond, Hawthorne House (Concord) –Rory
- The Mount (Edith Wharton's Estate) (Lenox) –Rory

Louisiana

- Hotel Monteleone & Carousel Bar (hosted William Faulkner, Truman Capote, Tennessee Williams, and Eudora Welty) (New Orleans) –Rory

Georgia

- Margaret Mitchell's House (Atlanta) –Rory

Alabama

- Zelda and F. Scott Fitzgerald Museum (Montgomery) –Lorelai and Rory

Mississippi

- Rowan Oak (William Faulkner House) (Oxford) –Rory

For New York Travel Recommendations, Turn to Chapter 11

Reading Recs around the World

Reading Lolita in Tehran: A Memoir in Books by Azar Nafisi (Iran)
A Moveable Feast by Ernest Hemingway (France)
A Passage to India by E. M. Forster (India)
A Room with a View by E. M. Forster (Italy and England)
The Sun Also Rises by Ernest Hemingway (Spain)
The Da Vinci Code by Dan Brown (France and England)

The Hunchback of Notre Dame by Victor Hugo (France)
Life of Pi by Yann Martel (India and Mexico)
One Hundred Years of Solitude by Gabriel García Márquez (Colombia)
The Gnostic Gospels by Elaine Pagels (Egypt)
On the Road by Jack Kerouac (United States)
Balzac and the Little Chinese Seamstress by Dai Sijie (China)
Galápagos by Kurt Vonnegut (Ecuador)

Gilmore Guidebook Recommendations :

Europe through the Back Door, 2003 by Rick Steves –Lorelai and Rory
The Rough Guide to Europe, 2003 Edition –Lorelai and Rory
Myra Waldo's Travel and Motoring Guide to Europe, 1978 by Myra Waldo –Emily and Richard

Amy's Untitled Mother-Daughter Show

On Writing and Creating Stories with Heart

"Songwriting is about making yourself open and vulnerable so the lyrics come out true."

—Zack on waiting for his muse (Sn 6 Ep 4)

You might think that the inspiration for a show that took over the pop culture scene, dominated the media over the past twenty-five years, and has an enduring quality would be born in a moment of glory. As discussed in the travel chapter, that moment is as rare as Emily Gilmore wearing jeans. Therefore, it's no surprise that *Gilmore Girls* did not start with that moment of idealized inspiration.

Amy Sherman-Palladino has recounted the tale of how the show was born, and it's not majestic in the least. Instead, it's an off-the-cuff response to a previously unfruitful pitch meeting. At the ATX Television Festival in 2015, Amy shared the details of one of her sessions at Warner Brothers and revealed they didn't go for any of her ideas. So, they asked what else she had, and Amy offered "a mother-daughter show where the mother and daughter are friends," a premise the WB bought immediately.

That simple, impromptu idea started the phenomenon. Sure, the concept was good, but as with all good ideas, it required something to make it great, something to catapult it into the stratosphere and stand out among a sea of other shows and media vying for viewers' attention.

To work on the pilot episode for her new show, Amy didn't just get a room of her own 📖; she got a magnificent Mayfair Inn of her own, using it and the town of Washington, Connecticut, to inspire the world of Stars Hollow and its colorful characters. Virginia Woolf may argue that attaining a distraction-free place to write led to the brilliance of *Gilmore Girls*, but I'm here to debate that it wasn't a makeshift writer's retreat that held the secret sauce: it was all truth, heart, and a pinch of atonement, three vital aspects of the creative process.

Let's start with the pilot episode. Minus the dialogue, scripts are bare-bones outlines when it comes to the rest of the scenery, action, costumes, etc.; it's not like reading a book, where an author can spend an entire page just describing the types of roads in Russia. 📖 In a script, every word counts. The script describes a "historical old town with white clapboard houses, huge trees, rolling hills, and no fences." Immediately, it's all charm and nostalgia, a picturesque New England town. But, for me, the last two words in that section are the ones that hold the greatest impact: "no fences."

For some reason, the American dream always seems to require the '50s-era white picket fence lifestyle, as seen in *Leave It to Beaver* 🎬 or *The Donna Reed Show*, 🎬 but that lifestyle, sitting behind its pristine fences, can also be exclusive. Amy wanted her dream world to be inviting and open to everyone. She wanted the viewer to feel at home and a part of the community from the very first second, a version of truth and heart that is often lacking in our modern culture, an atonement for the loneliness epidemic that currently pervades our world.

So, we have charm and inclusivity representing our themes of heart, truth, and atonement, but what makes up the rest of the *Gilmore* . . . je ne sais quoi?

On the second page of the pilot script, a young man hits on Lorelai and mentions he's passing through town. Of course, she calls him a Jack Kerouac. 📖 The script clearly states that this man has no idea what Lorelai is talking about, which sets the bar for the rest of the show, as only the most astute minds can understand what Lorelai and Rory are alluding to most of the time. The dialogue quickly goes on to mention RuPaul, Macy Gray, and Officer Krupke from *West Side Story* 🎬 —a slew of references quickly upping the intellectual ante of the show and its characters.

I've watched my fair share of TV shows, and the one thing *Gilmore Girls* does better than any show I've seen yet is pop culture references. The Rory Gilmore Reading Challenge alone names over four hundred works of literature. Add in the Movie Challenge (over three hundred titles) and the TV Challenge (over one hundred shows) and you're looking at a pop culture compendium of almost eight hundred entries. Razzlefrat, Bendelschnitz, am I right? Of course, the show also frequently mentions celebrities, politicians, musicians, historical figures, architects, and so many more. I'm not sure whether anyone has counted all those allusions, but I'm sure it's also a hefty list. *Gossip Girl* and *The West Wing* 🎬 may come close in number of references, but the pop culture crown goes to *Gilmore Girls*, no contest.

So why does this make for notable writing? And what does it have to do with the essential writing elements: heart and truth? First of all, this pop culture intelligence is an intrinsic part of these characters. So, you might say, it's part of their heart. Amy Sherman-Palladino has shared that she intentionally created Lorelai and Rory to be characters that were open to anything and everything, from the mainstream, like *Cinderella* and *Pinocchio*, to the obscure, like *The Peace of Nicias and the Sicilian Expedition*, and the bizarre, like *The Real Animal House.* She wanted them to be well-rounded people interested and engaged not just in their world of Stars Hollow but in the world at large. This connectivity is a significant truth of our world; we are all tied together by invisible strands of reference, whether we know it or not.

Let's journey back to England in the 1500s and 1600s when Shakespeare performed *The Merry Wives of Windsor* for Queen Elizabeth I, who put her stamp of approval on the play and shared it with the world. Then, four hundred years later, in 1909, Mark Twain was inspired by a visit from Helen Keller—yes, that Helen Keller—and because of their conversation, he put his satirical pen to the task of questioning the authorship of the plays attributed to William Shakespeare.

Another hundred years later, writer Amy Sherman-Palladino is vacationing in Connecticut, visiting Mark Twain's house (where the aforementioned meeting of the minds took place), and imagining what life in a small New England town would be like. Of course, that was the birth of *Gilmore Girls*. The show also includes twelve of Shakespeare's plays, four stories from Mark Twain, Helen Keller's autobiography, and Harriet Beecher Stowe's iconic tale, *Uncle Tom's Cabin.* (Stowe's house is next to Mark Twain's.)

Today, *Gilmore Girls* is watched by millions of people, including *Barbie* herself—Margot Robbie! Celebrated for her roles in *Suicide Squad, The Wolf of Wall Street,* and *I, Tonya*, Robbie is currently known worldwide for her portrayal of the iconic Mattel doll. While *IndieWire* reports that Proust Barbie was cut from the film because audiences didn't understand the reference, I'm certain that the joke would have landed with *Gilmore* fans who remember Max Medina's favorite series of books from Proust, In Search of Lost Time.

But the Gilmore/Barbie connection doesn't stop there. Robbie has shared that she used *Gilmore Girls*, Lorelai in particular, to help her prepare for her role as Barbie, which I understand completely. The themes of self-discovery, the power of women, and the use of pop culture to inform, educate, and inspire others are reflected in that show, and their references are also the tenets by which I create my art, my writing, and the very book you're reading now, my way of reflecting all the universal truths and moments of heart that I see in the world.

That's why reflecting *all* aspects of the world (race, gender, ability, etc.) is vital to creating books, TV shows, and movies. You never know who's watching, and you never know what influences will inspire the truth and heart of the current and future generations.

Truth and heart are why we all fall in love with an entirely fictional universe; we connect with emotions of the characters on the page and screen. I may not be the biggest fan of Stephen King or Ernest Hemingway, but there's one thing these authors, every book on writing, and I all agree on: to succeed, there must be truth in the writing. A work absent of truth will not attract and engage readers, it will not resonate with them, and in the end, it will have failed in its purpose.

Ironically, Jess Mariano, the Anthony Bourdain–esque bad boy of the book world, has the worst time with truth, heart, and atonement when he first arrives in Stars Hollow. But thank goodness for Luke, self-help books, and many life experiences because later in the series, Jess is laser focused on these three things. He openly admits his affection for the important people in his life (Luke and Rory)–a truth and heart combo. In a beautifully written character arc, older-but-wiser Jess sets boundaries, communicates his feelings, and focuses on what's genuine for him–a champion of truth. Finally, he writes Luke a check for all the times his uncle helped him out of trouble and makes up for his time of scalawagging and troublemaking with hard work at his publishing house and on writing his first novel. Say it with me: atonement. And there you have it, proof from the character development of Jess Mariano that atonement, truth, and heart are essential tools for the writer.

My journey with truth and heart started at an early age. Since I was young, I remember lying in bed at night flipping through the cerebral pages of stories I'd created in my head, trying to decide which tale to reimagine or flesh out in the quiet moments before the sandman whisked me off to sleep. Some stories had blossomed from the haziness of actual dreams, and others had just occurred to me as I stared into the darkness of my room. I didn't know it then, but I was already practicing honing my truth detector, zeroing in on the invisible intricacies that make us human: our thoughts, our desires, our emotions, our souls.

The entirety of my early work will probably never be published, or even written down, but I created what I felt and what I thought: my truths, my heart.

Just like Rory is initially uncertain about choosing Yale over her lifelong dream of going to Harvard, no major life decision is made without a few moments of hesitation. Throughout college and the after years, I questioned my ability and destiny to be a writer. Were my versions of truth and heart even worth putting on the page? No matter how much I faltered on my path or how long I abstained from writing, I always returned to honor the words that seemed to be written across my heart. As Ian McEwan describes in *Atonement*, "Writing was the thread of continuity. It was what she [Briony] had always done." It is what *I* have always done.

There's a standard line of advice that says, "Write what you know." Paris even says this to Rory in season seven! Many writers, myself included, have taken this instruction very literally, feeling boxed in by the current scope of our experiences and an overwhelming imposter syndrome when contemplating stepping outside society's previously established boundaries. Sometimes, this means a writer's work can be very autobiographical, each page an atonement for the life unlived, "The Road Not Taken," and the words unspoken. I've certainly dreamed up enough action-packed tales to atone for all the times I've been confined to my bed. Intentionally or unintentionally, each word, each sentence holds clues to the life of its creator, our souls seeping through the pen and into the letters on the page.

My creative writing courses, however, taught me that writing what I *knew* was more complicated than expected. In class, I wrote about things I loved (Christmas), things I cared about and believed in (family, friends, etc.). Some were fantastical, while others were about my real-life experiences. My instructors, however, urged me to write "their way," squeezing me into their mold of what a writer should be and criticizing every move I made. For them, an artist's goal was to shock, appall, stay within the accepted guidelines, replicate what had been done before like a good little *Clockwork Orange*, and accept a creative process that was not their own, but I didn't adhere to any of that. My writing philosophy meant staying true to my own truth and my own heart.

While I always worked diligently to improve my abilities as a writer, I was confident in my skills. Still, with so many people with more experience, accolades, and certifications telling me I wasn't who I thought I was, the threads of doubt began to weave their web around me.

After two years in the fiction writing program, I was beginning to lose my resolve. Every day was a fight to stay true to my voice, and every second of class was a struggle to adhere to their process. As a result, my writing and my self-assurance suffered. Before, I had felt that writing was a wonderful art form full of imagination, possibilities, and exploration. Now, I felt confused, frustrated, and rejected. I questioned my future as a writer, just like Rory did after Mitchum tells her she "doesn't have it." I knew I couldn't write like them, but if I couldn't write like me, then what was I doing?

Just as Jo March lost focus when she tried to please everyone by becoming her world's definition of a writer and ended up with hollow, exaggerated stories, I, too, lost my way. After I graduated from school, my writing journey was irregular and unfocused; I'm sure the trials I'd faced at school were still looming in the back of my mind, causing my literary hesitation. I knew I still wanted to write, but I needed to figure out *what* to write about or even what format to choose. Then, *Gilmore Girls* inspired me to start the Rory Gilmore Reading Challenge. Some of the books I had read previously, but many were new or were ones I had waited to read for years and just never got around to it. Then, the idea for the *Gilmore Book Club* blog was born.

What if I wrote about this enormous reading list, this fantastic show, and everything that happened to me along the way? People love books and *Gilmore Girls*, so why not combine them and add my thoughts, feelings, and experiences? At that point, I barely knew what I was going to write about for each book, but I knew that this was what I was meant to be doing; this was my writing path transformed and my way forward. My blog would give voice to all the truths and lessons I wanted to share and all the things I am still discovering.

There are days when I feel like I can barely string together a decent sentence, and thankfully, there are days when writing feels as easy and as good as taking a deep breath and filling your lungs with life-sustaining air. And I know that despite all the rejection I've faced and the pestering doubt, this is my destiny. It may take time, and I may never be the next Candace Bushnell, Emma McLaughlin, 📖 or Sue Grafton, 📖 but my work will find its audience because it's brimming with truth and heart, and that is what resonates so deeply with people.

Just like Lorelai is ready with life advice for Rory, Jo's father in *Little Women* 📖 reveals that truthful stories are more powerful and valuable than the rest. "That's the secret. . . . You wrote with no thought of fame or money, and put your heart into it." There you have it, my Gilmores: truth and heart.

The world has not always celebrated the truth, and that's one of the reasons why art is so important. It allows people to learn, grow, and think about the world the way it is now and how it could be. When there is truth in art, the audience will find it and connect with it. It's the reason people devote their lives to celebrating intergalactic space battles 🎬 and why the stories of handmaidens in red robes are so terrifying. No one can guarantee that this deep connection will happen all the time; creating art is always a leap of faith, but trust me—the right audience is out there, and they're open to seeing the truth.

For the majority of my writing, I've written it for a reason. Still, nothing in my repertoire has contained so much truth as the essays I've crafted while reading titles from the Rory Gilmore Reading Challenge. From the wit and heart of *Gilmore Girls* to the incredible works of literature that reveal insights and experiences from around the world to the revelations and ruminations of my own, each thread that stitches this project together is adorned with beads of truth. My intention is to ensure that those adornments of truth and heart are stitched onto every piece of fabric that will make up the quilt of this and my future work.

So, go out and find *your* truth. Don't be afraid to venture to where your heart is leading you. You may encounter some resistance, but hold tight to your purpose, because you will find people who resonate with the same truth. And whatever you do, whatever art you create, I encourage you to embroider it with atonement, heart, and truth because, as Amy Sherman-Palladino, Jess, and Jo have shown us, that is the secret to success.

Follow the truth, Gilmore.

Quotes from Writers about the Craft of Writing

"You learn best by reading a lot and writing a lot, and the most valuable lessons of all are the ones you teach yourself." –*On Writing* by Stephen King 📖

"Do not worry. . . . All you have to do is write one true sentence. Write the truest sentence that you know." –*A Moveable Feast* by Ernest Hemingway 📖

"[Writers]–at least the great ones–must articulate the universal truths of the heart rather than the received wisdom of the moment." –*Double Lives: American Writers' Friendships* by Richard Lingeman

"... a [writer] must have money and a room of her own if she is to write fiction." –*A Room of One's Own* by Virginia Woolf

"Nobody can counsel you and help you, nobody.... Go into yourself. Search for the reason that bid you write ... acknowledge to yourself whether you would have to die if it were denied you to write." –*Letters to a Young Poet* by Rainer Maria Rilke

"During the process, David [Foster Wallace] helped me understand, more deeply than I had before, that art is about rigor and precision." –*In the Land of Men* by Adrienne Miller

"I learned so much from Mario [Puzo], perhaps most importantly, the need to rewrite and keep rewriting.... He also impressed on me the value of using everything that is important in your personal life." –Introduction by Francis Ford Coppola for *The Godfather* by Mario Puzo

"Didion once told a participant in a writing seminar that to get through writer's block, you had to write one sentence, and then another, and then another. To be a writer, you must write." –*The World According to Joan Didion* by Evelyn McDonnell

"There's nothing to stop a man from writing unless that man stops himself. If a man truly desires to write, then he will. Rejection and ridicule will only strengthen him." –*The Captain Is Out to Lunch* by Charles Bukowski

"I honestly think in order to be a writer, you have to learn to be reverent. ... Let's think of reverence as awe, as presences in and openness to the world." –*Bird by Bird: Some Instructions on Writing and Life* by Anne Lamott

Ditching Darcy

Finding a Soulmate in Stars Hollow

"I feel like I'm never gonna have it. The whole package, you know? That person, that couple life . . . I really want it."

—Lorelai (Sn 3 Ep 1)

Stars Hollow was built on love, the kind of love that fairy tales (or Founders' Days tales) are made of. In a *Romeo and Juliet*–type story, two lovers from opposing towns run away to be together and find each other under the light of a constellation of stars, and the founders built the town of Stars Hollow on that romantic spot. Love is so integral to the history of Stars Hollow that it deserves its own wing in the Twickham House Museum.

We all know it takes more than wishing on a star to find such passion. As Lorelai wrote in her famous season seven letter to Rory regarding her reconciliation with Logan, "Love is elusive and all-encompassing; when you fall under its intoxicating spell, you have little recourse but to live out its devices." So, how do we find that all-encompassing love? And if we have it, how do we hold on to it? Clearly, the subject of true love brings up a lot of questions.

Like its fictional town, *Gilmore Girls* is deeply rooted in romantic relationships. The love of a Gilmore girl is an honor not to be taken lightly, not by the characters, not by the fans, and certainly not by me.

If you look at some of the most iconic shows over the years, the "will-they-won't-they" dynamic of two lead characters is one of the most critical factors in capturing the hearts and minds of an audience. I'm talking about shows like *Friends*, *Grey's Anatomy*, and *The Office*. This trope has nothing to do with the show's quality; all I'm saying is a good Ross and Rachel situation is like catnip for the viewers because there is nothing our society loves more than assuming a Poirot-like attention to detail in order to discover everything we can about love. Give us a Dr. McDreamy and a Meredith Grey and we're out of our minds obsessed.

In *Gilmore Girls*, that relationship was Lorelai and Luke. But the competition for Lorelai is rampant. The first time we see Lorelai in the pilot episode, it takes only two minutes for Luke to flirt with her in his adorably grumpy manner and for another guy to ask Lorelai out within the same scene. Those are impressive stats for any leading lady. Lorelai's flirtation with Chilton Dad? Just shy of six minutes into the second episode, about a minute after arriving at Chilton. Fifteen minutes into "The Deer Hunters," she's charming Max at Parents' Night. In the next episode, "Cinnamon's Wake," it takes only eight minutes to show Max asking Lorelai out. That's four different men over five episodes. If there's anyone to take dating advice from, it's Lorelai Gilmore. However, there's more to the topic than witty banter and a hair twirl, but more on that in a bit.

We also need to address the love quadrate of Rory Gilmore's romantic life. Now, Rory is newer to the dating scene and, therefore, a bit shy and slow to start. However, it soon turns into a four-person battle between

Rory and her love interests—Dean Forester, Jess Mariano, and Logan Huntzberger—that causes drama worthy of the viral book *He's Just Not That into You.*

As much as I wanted to enjoy their romances, Lorelai's and Rory's love lives often caused me anxiety; their lack of communication with their partners frustrated me to no end (and we'll discuss that further in this chapter). However, there are plenty of other relationships on the show that I'm incredibly fond of. It was beautiful watching Sookie marrying her mushroom man (Jackson), showing that people who had a unique personality and who didn't have the "default body" that's praised in magazines are worthy of love. Miss Patty and her four weddings, symbolizing that one should never give up on love. Liz and TJ, though eccentric at times, are enthusiastically supportive of one another; TJ is always talking up Liz's jewelry and how successful she is at this endeavor. Then, there's my favorite townie relationship: Babette and her husband, Morey, who are "Venus and a bowl of soup" kind of opposite, yet they adoringly embrace each other's interests and peculiarities. The message that everyone deserves love, no matter what they look like or how quirky they are, is a reminder of how our world should be and something I cling to when I anguish over my current relationship status.

When it comes to my love life, let's just say, get ready to find cats on my doorstep. Miss Patty would have loved to play Cupid for me at the Bid-on-a-Basket festival because I was alone and couldn't get my own guy. If the Gilmore girls are such a hot commodity and the townies are so involved in matchmaking, could they help me find my soulmate?

The question is easy, but the answer is a Facebook status: it's complicated. Although *Gilmore Girls* depicts its main characters as unique and desirable, and it seems like boys are always fighting over them, Lorelai and Rory don't always have a healthy love life. At times, they can be an excellent representation of what *not* to do in a relationship. I get that it makes for good TV, but viewers, myself included, don't always expertly separate the messages of what to do and what not to do that we absorb from our media, especially when it comes from two beloved characters such as Rory and Lorelai.

So, here's the Gilmore Digest version. The lessons boil down to two things: settling and communication.

As much as I love Luke and Lorelai and want Rory to have her ideal guy, I find that those couples tend to bring me less joy as I rewatch the series. Before you get upset, notice I said "less joy," not "no joy." Luke and Lorelai's first kiss at the Dragonfly test run with Kirk streaking by is still the best thing ever. What I mean is that I'm not looking at these couples as my be-all and end-all. Instead, I idolize Sookie and Jackson, Babette and Morey, and sometimes Emily and Richard as couples to show me what finding true love is like.

Do you know what these couples excel at? What is missing from Luke and Lorelai, and Rory and her trio of men? Communication! Yes, their inability to tell each other things makes for addicting TV, but it also makes for a bad relationship. Luke and Lorelai's time together is fraught with secrets: Luke hiding his daughter's existence from his fiancée for three months and Lorelai not telling Luke she's not comfortable with postponing the wedding. I could go on. As much as the Gilmore girls pride themselves on talking, they're rather awful at communicating what needs to be said, a frustratingly and beautifully ironic touch from the show's creator.

Rory and Jess are basically executives at Secrets-R-Us. Jess doesn't come clean about being unable to go to prom, the trouble he's having at school, and when he can't attend their previously made plans. Rory never opens up about how she feels about Jess blowing her off, how unsafe she sometimes feels with him, and how she can't count on him. Fortunately, Rory matures from this relationship, and even the one with Dean, and uses these experiences to enlighten her relationship with Logan. In this case, the depiction of Rory growing up gives the viewer valuable lessons in honesty, open communication, and the importance of getting what you need from a relationship.

Now, I can be a little too honest at times (like April), and I'm working to be better about that, but honesty is such an essential part of relationships—even when it's hard and even when it hurts. You can't have a relationship—any relationship, not just romantic ones—without honesty.

That takes us to our next romantic lesson on the pitfalls of settling. We could call Lynnie and set up a driveway therapy appointment, but she's currently in session at Six Flags, so I'll tell you what my therapist would say: you have to know what you want first.

Luckily, literature is replete with examples to choose from. *Tender Is the Night,* *The Great Gatsby,* *Wuthering Heights*, *The Red Tent,* and *Lady Chatterley's Lover* all revolve around those great loves and a definition of the right partner for someone. As a bibliophile, I've let the tales of Elizabeth and Darcy remain unquestioned for years, perfectly preserved as Snow White under her coffin of glass. After all, these stories are the "can't-eat, can't-sleep, reach-for-the-stars, over-the-fence, World Series kind of stuff" (yes, that's from *It Takes Two*). We're talking about the love of legends—the lovers that we still emulate, discuss, and analyze centuries later.

Is it because their love is so much greater than what we mortals experience? Or is it because the beloved is a model of human excellence, a paradigm of what a lover should be? Let's make it personal: If Max Medina sent one thousand yellow daisies to my workplace and asked me to spend the rest of my life with him, would I say yes and pick out my own Zelda Fitzgerald–inspired ring? I'm not so sure I would.

Until recently, culture has instructed people that their standards are too high, something others have told me repeatedly. We tell people to be more realistic. We roll our eyes when children tell us what they want in a partner instead of encouraging them to practice making and refining these choices. We lower our standards so that we get access to the exclusive world of couples, and then we wonder why things went wrong.

In contradiction to those beliefs, we have the highest possible standards for strangers, even for fictional characters like Lorelai and Rory.

In the second season of *Gilmore Girls,* Lorelai makes a heartbreaking but necessary decision concerning her fiancé, Max. Now, if there were a Darcy figure on *Gilmore Girls*, it's "Max, Medina, Max Medina." He's refined and intelligent, an expert at the witty banter part of flirting, devoted to educating and molding the young minds of the future, and steadfastly loyal to those he cares about. He's the perfect guy. But he's not perfect for Lorelai. It took her awhile, and God forbid, because of something her mother said, but Lorelai finally saw that. She does not want to try on her wedding dress every night and dream about her man like Emily did when she was a few days away from her wedding to Richard. And the audience gets it. We want Lorelai to have someone she's madly in love with, and that's not Max.

Lorelai may not have always been a reliable dating example for Rory, but this is one of Lorelai's best lessons: you deserve love, extraordinary love, and don't settle for anything less.

I know I've been critical of Rory in many scenarios, especially when she dates Dean for the second time (because Rory totally settled and made the safe, comfortable choice to go back to an old boyfriend, even though it was an unhealthy relationship and didn't meet the standards of her current life). Still, when looking at her relationship with Logan, I think Rory, to her benefit, has internalized Lorelai's example. In *Gilmore Girls*' final season, Logan proposes to Rory at her graduation party and Rory asks for some time to consider, leading to the hilarious turtle-bird conversation with Lorelai. This moment is a crucial turning point for Rory. She's not ready to move to San Francisco, to be married, or to begin her career as a trailing spouse at a newspaper not of her own choosing. As much as she loves Logan and their life together, Rory ultimately chooses herself.

I'm not sure the writers intended this to be another instance where Rory's life (turning down Logan) mirrors Lorelai's life (turning down Max), but I think it's a beautiful depiction not only of how Rory learns from Lorelai but also of how the Gilmore girls retain their individuality, that they choose to preserve that same spark that we all fell in love with. They decide to remain Gilmores. Gilmores have high standards, and while sometimes it can be challenging when it comes to having a relationship with yourself *and* one with a partner, having high standards is a good thing.

However, to have high standards, you must know what those standards are to identify them when they appear. You can't just say, "Where's my Luke?" and hope the next person serving your coffee is the one. It doesn't work like that. You have to be super, super specific about the characteristics you're looking for. You do have the right to change your standards, but make sure it's truly because you are changing, not because someone else wants you to change.

So, I'm going to give you an example. If I were to make up a list using my literary and pop culture knowledge to create my perfect man, here are the traits he would possess:

- Mr. Darcy's bookish devotions and extreme loyalty
- John Thornton's honesty, passion, and directness (if he has a voice like Richard Armitage, that's a plus)
- Aragorn's leadership skills

- Neville's loyalty and hard work and, of course, his ability to Longbottom (go look that up if you need to)
- Derek Shepherd's faith in love and in the people around him
- Colin Bridgerton's ability to charm and converse with anyone (book Colin, not TV Colin)

And, of course, the Gilmore traits:

- Dean's certainty in pursuing the shy girl and embracing her quirks
- Jess's literary references, his communication skills (later in the series), and his ability to identify, support, and celebrate people's true passions
- Luke's chef status, readiness to help in any situation, and thoughtful gestures
- Jackson's devotion (find a guy who will sleep with the zucchini just to make sure your soup is the best it can be and you will find a guy whose commitment will outlast the rest)
- Logan's lightheartedness and spontaneity (but only like a teeny-tiny drop of this)
- Max's intelligence, wit, and ability to communicate

And presto—the perfect man!

Except there is no perfect man because there are no perfect people. There aren't even perfect people in books or TV shows because we wouldn't be attracted to or identify with them.

There are many reasons we idolize Luke and Lorelai, why their relationship has such an impact on the hearts of fans. We love their chemistry, their back-and-forth, and their embodiment of the hope that friendship can blossom into love. However, all these traits were specially crafted for these characters. A group of writers and producers sat around thinking about the attributes of one person and created complementary characteristics in another person so they'd match perfectly. As writers, we are the hands of fate, Cupid's arrows, and the winds of destiny. We may treat characters like people, listening to their wants and needs, but ultimately, something within a writer's heart and mind has put all of that into being.

Even though Lorelai and Luke's relationship was so carefully crafted, it was still rife with the mistakes and messiness that make us human.

So, let me reiterate that we're not looking for perfect people; we're looking for people who are perfect for who we are. We are not looking for an exact Luke replica; we are looking for our own version of Luke.

At one point, I may have needed Luke or Darcy to give me someone to hope for and dream about, and if that's where you are right now, that's great. But going through this Gilmore TED Talk on love has taught me that when it comes to my soulmate, not only do I not need the aforementioned romantic icons for myself, I don't want them. I can use them for inspiration when deciding on what I want and appreciate the lessons they've taught me, but that's where their involvement in my romantic life ends.

I need to own the creation of my romantic relationships and not use someone else's template that was specifically created for someone else's needs and personality. I want my own hero–someone who couldn't be separated from me if tempted by all the literary and TV heroines ever created because the universe wrote my partner into existence for me and me alone.

You deserve to find that person too. I know the process can feel frustrating and fraught with opportunities for mistakes, but remember, not even Lorelai and Rory are perfect. You don't have to be perfect to be worthy of love. All you have to do is be your best, authentic self and clearly define what you want in a partner. Don't get distracted by someone who doesn't meet your standards, because you deserve the best. And last but not least, keep the commandment of communication, because that is how you find and keep the Luke to your Lorelai or the Morey to your Babette!

You are worthy of all-encompassing love, Gilmore!

Deleted Scene Summary: Season 2, Episode 1 "Sadie, Sadie"

Flowers for Algernon 📖 and daisies for Lorelai. After Max's proposal, the town of Stars Hollow shows up at the Gilmores' to choose a bouquet for themselves from the profusion of flowers now residing in the Gilmore living room and hallway. To help Lorelai determine whether she should marry Max, Rory makes up one of her classic pro-con lists. There is a staggering number of notes in the pro column, including "an excellent vocabulary," "extensive knowledge of famous women in literature," and "showers frequently," but Rory has nothing in the con category. Lorelai notes that he has a pair of elephant boxer shorts, which are definitely a con, but Rory insists that Lorelai take this exercise seriously because this decision will affect both of their lives.

Behind the Scenes: Cast Members Dating Other Cast Members

Rory and Jess were a couple in real life! Alexis Bledel and Milo Ventimiglia dated for almost four years (or three years, depending on which magazine you read). Although they broke up in 2006, the fans enjoyed the idea of a Rory and Jess relationship being a real thing. There were also rumors of Alexis dating Jared Padalecki, but nothing was confirmed until almost twenty years later; Padalecki told *Glamour* that he and Alexis briefly, and somewhat tamely, dated during the first season of *Gilmore Girls*.

Where there is Melissa McCarthy, there is Ben Falcone. It's true now, and it was true then. Two years before Melissa and Ben were married in 2005, Ben appeared on *Gilmore Girls* as Mr. Brink; yes, I had to look it up to find the character's name. Mr. Brink is Fran's lawyer with whom Lorelai and Sookie arranged to buy the Dragonfly Inn. According to *People*, this was the first time Melissa and Ben were in a scene together, and they clearly liked it so much that they continue to appear in or work on each other's projects to this day.

The hilarious Alex Borstein was initially scheduled to play Sookie, who later marries Jackson Belleville on the show. Ironically, Alex's then-husband, Jackson Douglas, was cast as Jackson Belleville and would have played the husband to his actual wife at the time. However, Alex was under contract elsewhere and had to pass on the role. Luckily for us, she did make a few appearances in the first season of *Gilmore Girls* as the sarcastic harp player, Drella, and in later seasons as Miss Celine, Emily and Richard Gilmore's stylist.

Straight for the Algonquin

On Creating Your Community

"It'll be like an online version of the Algonquin group, like throwing a party in your head, where everyone you've ever wanted to talk to is there."

—Rory (Sn 7 Ep 5)

There's no doubt that Lorelai is at home in her new community of Stars Hollow. From planning weddings at the Independence Inn to her morning coffee at Luke's to attending whatever festival the town is hosting, Lorelai has found her place. She loves that the bank teller can't count and that she knows the names of her neighbors' garden gnomes. She feels absolutely at ease and can see she's on the path to her desired future and that involves staying in Stars Hollow. Now that Lorelai's found her community, she never wants to leave.

But what is a community? Is it the people? The place? A particular building? I think it can be any and all of them. It can be just one person or many, a bunch of little different societies, or one big one. The important thing is that your community makes you feel supported and comfortable.

However, I also think your network of people should push you to grow a little. For example, Luke is there as a sounding board for Lorelai when she's freaking out over Dean kissing Rory. Luke even reminds Lorelai that she can't go after Dean, though he uses double coupon day at Doose's as an excuse; Luke knows that Lorelai just needs to talk it out and cool off before addressing the situation. Sookie also gently encourages Lorelai to pursue new relationships when she gets stuck in her couch-potato-girl ways. And Taylor, well, Taylor keeps everyone on their toes.

Of course, a community is also a source of help when needed. Mia helped Lorelai when she first needed a job and a place to live. Sookie assists Lorelai in sorting all the donations for the town rummage sale. Patty and Babette take turns watching and feeding Paul Anka, the dog, when Lorelai can't make it home. But a community isn't just one-sided; help requires reciprocation at some point. Lorelai signs up to make the costumes for the middle school's *Fiddler on the Roof* play, creates ornaments for the Firelight Festival, and sews one-of-a-kind colonial costumes for the "woman of questionable morals" town reenactment. She also babysits Martha and Davey for Sookie and Jackson when they want to go on their ski trip. Stars Hollow is a strong community because it is brimming with helping hands.

And finally, community is company. It's Sookie and Lorelai hanging out at home watching all three *A Star Is Borns*. 🎬 It's Gypsy and Jackson cracking jokes while looking for leftover Easter eggs. It's every person in the town attending a wake for Babette and Morey's cat, bringing over food, giving them hugs, and listening to Morey play the piano. A community doesn't need to do something big and flashy; they're there simply to enjoy being in your presence.

As much as we all want to fall in love with a Luke of our own or fulfill our inn-owning dreams, the community aspect of *Gilmore Girls* is what many fans desire the most. There have been many times when I've wished someone would run my errands with me just to keep me company, hang out and watch movies, or watch my cat when I go out of town. Finding a community in a small town like Stars Hollow can be pretty easy, especially with someone super friendly like Babette as your neighbor, but finding one in a big city like New York is something else altogether. I may have had some of the community aspects described above in my hometown in South Carolina, but I encountered what I will now call "the Rory problem."

Rory may have had people to hang out with and look out for her in Stars Hollow, but that was a community that she inherited, a community Lorelai built. Sure, Rory had a support system there, but finding your own place in the world is integral to growing up. Rory eventually found her place at Chilton, working on the paper and becoming student body vice president. With a bit of help from Lorelai, Rory also began to make friends at Chilton and discovered her rhythm at the *Yale Daily News*. However, school is a community for students for only so long. Eventually, you must go out into the wide, wide world and find your community for yourself. The series ends with Rory leaving Stars Hollow to follow Barack Obama's campaign, so we don't see how Rory fares after graduation. However, I believe her nomadic existence in *A Year in the Life* proves that Rory never found her community, and subconsciously, she fears she never will.

There's a scene in *Gilmore Girls*' final season where Rory has a dream reflecting her anxieties about graduating from Yale and entering the real world. In the dream, she is kicked out of Chilton and returns to find

Lorelai leaving indefinitely for Hawaii. Paris now owns Lorelai's house; even though it will always be Rory's home in her heart, it physically belongs to Paris. Plus, all of Rory's career dreams are smashed; her role in life is to keep picking up trash on the side of the road. The dream leaves Rory with a heightened sense of loss and a profound desire to find her place in the world.

As Rory grows up and moves forward with her life, she leaves the familiarity of her communities again and again: Chilton, Yale, the *Daily News*, Lorelai's house, and the biggest one, Lorelai herself. Rory's attempts to find a new home (*The New York Times,* the *Stamford Eagle Gazette,* the *Chicago Sun-Times, The Providence Journal-Bulletin*) don't pan out either. Cue meltdowns like sleeping with Dean, stealing a yacht, or blanking during her final exams and taking home the blue test book she was supposed to turn in. It's no wonder Rory is experiencing such ferocious emotional tremors; without our communities, we are untethered, disconnected, and lost in the abyss that is the wide, wide world.

We need our communities to keep us grounded and supported, to keep us in tune with who we are. Just look at how Rory gets through her breakdown: an infusion of home and community. It's not said like that on the show, but that's precisely what it is. She goes back to Lorelai's house, to where she grew up, and Lorelai devises a plan of iconic Stars Hollow activities (Luke's Diner, shopping, karaoke at KC's). With that combination of soothing activities and more quality time with Lorelai, Rory quickly starts feeling more like herself.

Just like Rory left Stars Hollow, I left my hometown to seek my fortune in big cities. I started with college in Chicago, then did a year in LA before deciding on moving to New York City. My sister had recently relocated to NYC, and since it was a big city with a nice, cold winter, I decided to move there, too, but without a job or a rock-solid plan of what I would do. My life was one big question mark at the time, and for some reason I couldn't put my finger on, I just knew New York was the answer.

For most of my childhood, my dreams seemed to exist far away in an unattainable universe. But in Chicago, and more so in NYC, it felt as if my dreams descended from the heavens to linger just slightly beyond my grasp, their closer proximity giving me hope. All I had to do was reach, and one day, I could hold their starlight in my hands. It may seem like a vague aspect of this topic, but I need my extended community to have the possibility of helping me accomplish my dreams, and I think that's why I immediately felt so at home in New York.

If I were to make a classic Rory pro-con list, my pro section for New York would far outweigh the cons. There's inspiration everywhere: art, fashion, architecture, events, exhibits, theater, libraries, TV and movie sets, and did I mention fashion and libraries? But there's also history here, a history of legends: financial tycoons, word wizards, renowned designers, US First Ladies, and titans of all industries. For so many big dreamers, all roads led to New York.

New York has literature written into its foundation. Herman Melville, Edith Wharton, Edgar Allan Poe, Joan Didion, Mark Twain, Simone de Beauvoir, J. D. Salinger, Ayn Rand, Dorothy Parker, and Truman Capote, to name a few, "and who each night, separately and together, were summoning me to their incomparable vocation" (*Sophie's Choice*). Many of these writers are also listed on the Rory Gilmore Reading Challenge. (Coincidence? I think not!) And why New York? Apparently, "that's where all writers go to get famous," according to Allison from *Peyton Place*. So many writers lived here at some point in their careers, and many call this city their home today.

That history is important to me; this is a city of writers, a city of books, a city of my people. That's where I want to write and the home I want for my literary career. That's the community I want to be a part of. I know that many of the people I've mentioned are dead, and the rest of them are complete strangers, but it's the atmosphere of dreamers that forms the foundation of my desired community.

Most people think having personal connections is the basis of community, and that's totally understandable. But I've always struggled with forming those relationships, much like Rory, and I've moved from city to city year after year where I didn't know anyone and had to start all over again. So, I don't mind that my community building began with the overall vibe rather than the individual people.

I don't think of New York as just my physical home. It's the home of all my dreams: my career, my friendships, my romantic relationships, my experience. It holds some of my favorite communities: the New York Public Library and the new Stavros Library, both of which I visit about once a week. And, of course, the Morgan Library and Strand Bookstore. A museum or public library may not seem like the place to find community, but for book lovers like me and Rory, it is. One day, I was with a friend and told her how off I was feeling. (No, Michel, it was not ennui.) We went through several areas of my life to try to determine where this feeling originated, but we couldn't get to the source. Luckily for me, we were heading to the Morgan Library, the ornate personal library–turned–museum of financier J. P. Morgan. The minute we stepped foot into the burgundy-paneled office lined with shelves of old books, I could feel the anxiety in my body evaporate. There are many definitions of community, but to me, this is it. It's a place or a person with whom I feel at peace, where I can be rejuvenated, refreshed, and inspired and be loved just as I am. It's all the "wild promise of all the mysteries and the beauty in the world" (*The Great Gatsby* 📖).

Now that I have the foundation, the "place" part, of my community, I'm working on building the rest: the company and camaraderie, the support, the help, the gentle push to grow. I've found a beautiful, loving kinship in Chronicon, an online community for people with a chronic illness. Though we mostly meet via the magic of the internet, this group is still a valued part of my life and has brought me comfort and support in so many ways. I'm also just starting to venture into the New York literary world, working on growing my community there, fostering friendships and working relationships with agents, authors, editors, publishers, illustrators, and more: my own little Algonquin group (with more manners and less drunken tirades). Plus, many curated groups that are specifically designed to help New Yorkers meet like-minded people have arisen from the social estrangement epidemic (much of that due to COVID), and I'm looking forward to taking part in those events. Physically meeting people isn't always something I'm particularly good at due to my introverted personality and the reduced mobility of my illness, but I'm working on making new friends in ways that are social but meet my needs as well. And together, the Gilmores, New York, and I will make my community dreams come true. Because what I tackle, I conquer.

It's complicated and takes a frustrating amount of time to build a well-rounded community, but remember, the Lorelai we meet in the pilot episode has been in Stars Hollow for years and has had the time to build up all these relationships. We later find out that she didn't know as many people when she first moved to town, such as Luke and his then-girlfriend, Rachel, because Lorelai was busy with a young daughter. If Lorelai can build a community in a place where she knew no one, so can you.

It doesn't matter whether you just moved to a new city or have lived there your whole life and are just looking for new ways to engage with people; a community can be formed anywhere at any time. In fact, I can thank the Gilmores for the newest friendship in my life. I was working as background on a set and the person next to me saw the Luke's mug photo that I had as the lock screen on my phone. Of course, we started talking all things *Gilmore Girls* and transitioned our connection from work friends to real friends. It just goes to show community can happen when you least expect it.

I still have my home in my family and my friends who aren't physically in NY; there is, after all, this thing called a phone where I can talk to them any time I want. But now, I'm beginning to build the rest of the equation. I'm continually searching for communities that accept me for who I am, that support me, and that cherish me. However, I also know I need that community to push me to grow and to offer help when I need it and, of course, offer their company for everything from movie nights to town festivals. It's never easy to build such a community, but even the small experiences I've had with finding my people prove that finding the *right* community is always worth it. I hope you all find that community or many because a true community is a blessing we all deserve.

Go find your people, Gilmore!

Gilmore Girls Quotes from Celebrity Fans

Check out these famous fans who can't get enough of Rory and Lorelai.

"I've been obsessed with the show since it came out. It helped shape Barbie, especially Lorelai. It was so incredible to use one of my all-time favorite characters as an inspiration." –Margot Robbie (*Vogue*)

"The amount of jealousy running through me is astounding Love. Me. Some. *Gilmore Girls*." –Kelly Clarkson replying to a fan pic of the Stars Hollow Sign on X

"Would you consider doing a *Gilmore Girls* musical? Just asking for a friend . . . I just wanna see Luke dancing . . . I think people would love it!" –Kelly Clarkson to Lauren Graham on *The Kelly Clarkson Show*

Kelly Clarkson also performed "Where You Lead" with Carole King for the 2019 Global Citizen Festival in New York.

"This is where my brain explodes: I go from supernerdy superfan to on-set talking to Lorelai Gilmore. It was my favorite show of all time. I was totally obsessed with it." –Sutton Foster on being in *Gilmore Girls: A Year in the Life* (*People*)

"I said that I watch *Gilmore Girls* every night before I go to bed. And it's true. It's so good. . . . A lot of people online were like, hey, are you a real fan? And I actually am a giant fan. I'm team Jess." Jimmy goes on to name his top four favorite characters (minus Lorelai and Rory): 1. Paris 2. Kirk 3. Luke 4. Taylor (He later names Sookie as the invisible number 5.) –Jimmy Fallon on *The Tonight Show Starring Jimmy Fallon*

"*Gilmore Girls* is a timeless treasure." –Mara Wilson on X

"I think about Lorelai all the time. I think about [Sookie's] produce, you're very particular about your produce!" –Mark Consuelos during a *Live with Kelly and Mark* interview with Melissa McCarthy. Kelly even revealed Mark is in a group chat called "The Gilmore Girlers" with his nieces so they can discuss the show.

"I was in my room, trying not to hyperventilate, just watching *Gilmore Girls* to try and take my mind off it." –British runner Phoebe Gill on how she dealt with nerves during the Paris 2024 Olympics (*The Independent*)

Gilmore Guide to New York City

Lorelai plans a perfect day in New York to celebrate Rory going to Yale; her choices are all listed below. However, I've also added a few places that I love and a few inspired by other Gilmore characters (marked with an *) for the perfect NYC itinerary.

Manhattan

- Strand Bookstore–Rory and Paris
- New York Public Library and the Morgan Library*–Rory, Richard, and Paris

* Not explicitly mentioned in the show, but the character would love and recommend

- Pizza at John's–Lorelai and Rory
- The Metropolitan Museum*–Rory
- A Broadway show–Lorelai
- Rough Trade record store*–Jess and Lane
- Tea at the Plaza Hotel*–Emily
- The Carnegie Diner*–Luke

Brooklyn

- Coney Island–Richard (Emily under protest)
- Brooklyn Flea*–Mrs. Kim
- Bushwick Collective Street Art*–Jess

Queens

- Socrates Sculpture Park*–Lucy and Olivia
- Mets game at Citi Field*–Luke
- Museum of the Moving Image*–Lorelai

Bronx

- New York Botanical Garden*–Emily and Richard
- Yankee Stadium*–Luke

Staten Island

- Alice Austen House*–Rachel
- Cookie Jar* (for cookies and unique cookie jars)–Lorelai

* Not explicitly mentioned in the show, but the character would love and recommend

The Reigning Gilmores

Iconic Women and Their Lasting Influence

"Gloria Steinem would be so proud."

—Rory (Sn 7 Ep 14)

If you could have your very own Friday Night Dinner with anyone, dead or alive, from any time or place, who would it be? It's a timeless question asked at social gatherings, in Instagram captions, and in celebrity interviews. We know Rory's idols–Hillary Clinton, Christiane Amanpour, and Isabel Allende–so I feel confident she'd like to share a meal with them, but her list of role models is extensive, so it's hard to narrow down her choice. Imagining Lorelai's dining companion gives us far more creative options like the Bangles or Patti Smith. Emily might also have some good answers: Jackie Kennedy or Emily Post (haha!). As much as I envision Richard wanting to meet with a historical icon such as Plato or a thinker like Nietzsche, I think he'd exchange a hundred meetings with these legends to have dinner one more time with his mother, Trix (Lorelai I). This dinner exercise may seem unrelated, but it represents the influence iconic women had in the characters' lives as well as our own and how to use their lessons when considering our own legacies.

While I'd want to have dinner with anyone from the Gilmore cast and the Palladinos, my go-to answer has always been (and probably always will be) Queen Elizabeth I. I've devoured every book, movie, and show I could find about the English monarch, and I still want more. I want to know everything that made Queen Bess so strong, what helped her endure, what advice she'd give to a modern woman, and how she dealt with the men who wanted to control her power.

Gilmore Girls is the pinnacle of girl power—the feminine reference is even there in the title! Written and sometimes even directed by Amy Sherman-Palladino, led by a cast of unforgettable female characters and references to iconic women (which we'll get into in a bit), the show is supported by an incredible list of female writers, directors, producers, editors, costumers, musicians, and many more artists who contributed, a testament to the incredible women who populate our universe. I know how difficult it can be to break into a male-dominated industry, and the TV/film world can be very exclusive based on gender (and other biases), so it's wonderful to see a show brimming with amazing women in front of and behind the camera.

For me, this show is an example of the art we can create when all voices are heard and everyone is given an opportunity. While it's disheartening to take in all the examples of inequality, it can also be inspiring to take a deeper look at those who have come before and paved the way for the future. After all, isn't that one of the foundations of *Gilmore Girls*? Rory looking up to Lorelai and all her other idols and wanting to be like them, to carry on the work they started?

In preparation for this book, I've done plenty of research. Of course, I've watched the show a lot, but I've also examined all aspects of the series, from looking at the crew list of the camera department to reading *Daughter of Fortune* and researching authors from the Rory list, like Agatha Christie and her famous disappearance. It's been humbling to see the incredible work and influence of these women and imagine how I can continue their legacy and pay it forward for the next generation. But if I hadn't been writing this book, I'm not sure I would've been learning as much about the dedication and bravery of these heroines and giving them the honor they deserve.

When I was young, I had what you could call a young adult Shakespeare book, an easy prose version of all his plays, like *Othello* and *Julius Caesar*, and it was one of my favorites. Looking at my bookshelves now, you will find all of Jane Austen's books, Shakespeare's sonnets, Keats's poems, and the Brontës. All British writers. Just like Paris Geller, I can be "quite the Anglophile" (Sn 4 Ep 12).

Once again, *Gilmore Girls* stepped in and changed my perspective. While the show is created by and portrays a multitude of women, which is wonderful to see, it's always important to take a look at what we could do better, and the pop culture lists that the show inspired could certainly improve. Of the over four hundred books on the Rory Gilmore Reading Challenge list, only twenty-five percent of the titles have female authors. Even worse, only two Black authors are named, and only a handful of writers are not of European or American descent. Not good, my friends, not good. As I read through the book list and paid more attention to the references on the show, I began to compare my literary and cultural awareness with what I saw on the reading list and in the world around me. I realized just how unintentionally narrow my field of vision had become. Just like Paris would benefit from reading outside her British comfort zone, I, too, could do better. I needed to start taking in the entire world's worth of stories, lessons, and people that deserve my respect as equally as those I've already mentioned.

At the very least, I should be learning about women from my own country, about the people who directly and indirectly shaped the life I live. I should be exploring the works of women like Susan Faludi, Elizabeth Wurtzel, and Judith Butler, who challenge society's gender rules. I should be enjoying *Oryx and Crake* by Margaret Atwood, *A Bolt from the Blue and Other Essays* by Mary McCarthy, *The Lottery: And Other Stories* by Shirley Jackson, and *The Lovely Bones* by Alice Sebold. I should be learning about influential women by studying *Living History* by Hillary Clinton, *Savage Beauty: The Life of Edna St. Vincent Millay* by Nancy Milford, and the letters and novels of Dawn Powell. Basically, I need to be better at diversifying my bookshelves. The Rory Gilmore Reading Challenge may have pushed me outside my *genre* comfort zone, but I need to take this lesson to the next level by embracing the stories from my own country *and* tales from marginalized groups, both of which are lacking in the Rory list.

Rory and Lorelai want to experience the whole enchilada, and that's the mindset I want to emulate. They discuss everything from *Swimming with Giants: My Encounters with Whales, Dolphins and Seals* to *Angela's Ashes* to *Secrets of the Flesh: A Life of Colette.* And they don't shy away from serious or uncomfortable subjects either. I'm not a fan of how Rory and Lorelai joke about Sylvia Plath because mental health and the ramifications of ignoring one's well-being should be taken seriously. However, I believe it's vital to experience conversations on the female psyche and mental health with *The Bell Jar* and Plath's journals, *Sybil* by Flora Rheta Schreiber, and *Girl, Interrupted* by Susanna Kaysen. I am glad that *Gilmore* is indirectly bringing this topic and others to the forefront by referencing these books and I intend to do my part in paying that education forward.

I can't change the books the characters referenced on *Gilmore Girls*, but I can change the way I discuss the show and how I encourage fans to interact and engage with the material. That's a large part of the inspiration for this book. It's also why I make book lists for what Lorelai and Rory would be reading today, continuing the conversation and engagement in the fandom but also diversifying the content so it helps fans explore marginalized authors and literature. This diversifying practice helps adapt *Gilmore Girls* and all its goodness to the current culture and bring it into the modern world.

I know you might be thinking, "Lady, I barely have time to shower, let alone read an entire library's worth of books." I hear you! That's why I'm going to put my book nerd superpowers to work for you. There are endless lessons to learn from studying iconic women, but from everything I've learned, there are two things that I've found over and over in each of these women's stories: perseverance against all odds and steadfast dedication to a cause or each other. Some of my favorite examples are below, so when you need a boost, the strength of these iconic women is here to help you keep going, and when you're able, you can pass this knowledge along.

Perseverance

Rory Gilmore always wanted to be a journalist, but after newspaper expert Mitchum Huntzberger tells her she doesn't have what it takes, Rory starts to believe she's not good enough. However, she perseveres, going back to Yale and working hard to graduate on time, achieving the title of editor of the *Yale Daily News*, and graduating with a job offer to be a reporter on Barack Obama's presidential campaign.

And now for some real-life examples:

Mary Rodgers started writing music at sixteen, later using her perseverance in her craft to transition her writing from musicals like *Once upon a Mattress* to books like *Freaky Friday*.

Pregnant and battling breast cancer, **Rachel Howzell Hall** struggled in a multitude of ways. Her first book, *A Quiet Storm,* had found a publisher, but rejection letters poured in for her next book, the Detective Elouise Norton series. Though Hall debated giving up, she never stopped writing. After other books and more surgeries, Hall finally found an editor who said yes to Detective Norton.

While many writers start out as devoted readers, it's not always the case. **Andrea Levy**, author of *Small Island,* lacked an interest in reading until she picked up *The Women's Room* by Marilyn French and books by Toni Morrison and Alice Walker. She worked with writing tutors and, of course, read more books until she became a published writer herself. Her first book, *Every Light in the House Burnin',* was published in 1994.

Laura Hillenbrand experienced pain and fatigue so debilitating she dropped out of college to manage her symptoms (later diagnosed as chronic fatigue syndrome). Hillenbrand didn't give up on her dreams. She continued to write, describing in her *New Yorker* essay that she often conducted phone interviews for *Equus* and wrote articles from bed, even writing with her eyes closed when overcome with dizziness. After years of hard work and incredible perseverance, she published *Seabiscuit: An American Legend* in 1999, which became a *New York Times* bestseller and the basis for the 2003 movie starring Tobey Maguire.

Dedication

Lorelai Gilmore is the definition of dedication when it comes to being a mom. When Rory was young, Lorelai held Rory's hands all night when she had chicken pox so Rory wouldn't scratch herself and get scars. Lorelai also spends the entire night in a chair by Rory's bed just in case she's needed the first night after Rory fractures her wrist.

Let's take a look at some real-life examples:

Did you know **Isabell Allende** (*Eva Luna,* *Daughter of Fortune,* and *The House of the Spirits*) sits down to write a new book every year on January 8? That's a woman who is dedicated to her craft.

Barbara Kingsolver, author of *Animal, Vegetable, Miracle,* worked as an art class model, typist, housecleaner, typesetter, and lab tech and assisted on archaeological digs in France and England to support herself before she became successful as a writer. She may not have known it at the time, but all of these occupations helped her become the dedicated writer she is today and showed her just how much hard work is a part of success.

Ann Patchett, author of *Bel Canto* and *Truth & Beauty: A Friendship,* met **Lucy Grealy**, author of *Autobiography of a Face,* in college. For over twenty years, the two embodied the meaning of a steadfast friendship. Through writing books, multiple surgeries, divorce, and addiction, these friends showed the world that our dedication to each other can make all the difference in the world.

Jodi Picoult, the author of *My Sister's Keeper,* admitted to the *New York Times Sunday Book Review* that she struggles with reading Russian novels (see, everyone has genres that aren't their favorite). However, she's still dedicated to the world of literature; she's a voracious reader of Toni Morrison, Alice Hoffman, and Mary Morris.

Despite her hydrocephalus diagnosis in her later years, **Mary McCarthy** (*The Group*) continued to pen her memoirs, studied Gothic architecture, and taught literature at Bard College. Now that's dedication to literature and to life!

Dedicated to helping people *Thrive,* **Arianna Huffington** founded Thrive Global in 2016 to help raise awareness about burnout. She's also penned fifteen books, including *The Sleep Revolution* and *Pigs at the Trough.*

"She continues to haunt our memories and inspire our days because she never gave up on life; she never stopped learning and changing . . ."

—*Eleanor Roosevelt: The Early Years* by Blanche Wiesen Cook 

Though Julia de Burgos left Puerto Rico at age twenty-five and never returned, she continued to show her dedication to her homeland by writing about its history and culture in her poems, *Song of the Simple Truth: Complete Poems.*

To all the women who have come before, to all those who are now, and to those in the future, I thank you. Your dedication and perseverance have made a difference in our world and have impacted countless lives, including mine. You chose to forge ahead through formidable terrain, not because you saw the action as brave but because you saw it as necessary, because you knew it to be the best path to a better world.

By focusing on female characters and relationships, employing women across its production departments, and referencing iconic women, *Gilmore Girls* has given us so many girl-power moments to enjoy, but for me, and for you, that's just the start. From all three Lorelai Gilmores to Laura Ingalls Wilder, Mary Roach, and P. L. Travers, the dedication, perseverance, and more lessons of other iconic women are an inspiration to us all.

It's breaking that universal mold that makes them, and any other woman for that matter, special. We revere and love those who dared to be different, for in our differences, there is immeasurable beauty. This is my vow to be better, to open my heart and mind to what women throughout the world and throughout time have to teach me, to diversify the stories I take in and the people I idolize, and to be the Gilmore I want to see in the world. And I hope after reading this chapter, you're inspired to do the same.

Keep marching on, Gilmore!

List of Iconic Female Cameos in Gilmore Girls

Madeleine Albright

In addition to serving as the first female US secretary of state and US ambassador to the United Nations, Albright appeared in *Gilmore Girls* in season seven, episode seven, in a scene re-creating Lorelai telling Rory about the night she was born.

Christiane Amanpour

Playing herself, the "glamourous, international war correspondent," Amanpour stays at the Dragonfly in the series finale. She meets Rory, who's in her pajamas, and has a quick conversation about Rory's journalistic aspirations.

Carole King

Grammy Award winner, Songwriters Hall of Fame member, and Rock and Roll Hall of Fame inductee, Carole King has made twenty-five solo albums, but Gilmore fans know her for writing and singing the *Gilmore Girls* theme song, "Where You Lead." King also appeared on the show for three episodes as music shop owner Sophie Bloom.

Melora Hardin

Famous for her roles on hit shows like *The Office,* the actress appeared in the final season of *Gilmore Girls* as therapist Carolyn Bates ("'Lynnie' to those in the know"), who helps Lorelai realize her relationship with Luke isn't what she wants.

Jane Lynch

What hasn't this comedian done? She's hosted game shows, voiced animated characters, and made cameos on everything from *Only Murders in the Building* to *Will & Grace*. However, Gilmore fans will never forget her role in season one, episode ten, as the nurse who deals with Emily and Lorelai at the hospital during Richard's heart attack.

Alex Borstein

Beloved for her work in *Family Guy* and *The Marvelous Mrs. Maisel*, Borstein appears in season one as Drella, the sassy harpist at the Independence Inn, and in seasons three and five as Miss Celine, the Gilmores' fashion consultant.

Other Famous Female Yale Graduates

Meryl Streep

"You'll have the best on-campus productions. You'll get to see the next Meryl Streep all goofy and eighteen and doing crap like 'Hey, name an occupation.'"

—Lorelai on pro-con for Yale (Sn 3 Ep 17)

Hillary Clinton

"And I already have my essay topic picked out . . . Hillary Clinton. She's so smart and tough and nobody thought she could win New York, but she did!"

—Rory (Sn 3 Ep 3)

Jodie Foster

Emily: "It's a panic room."

Lorelai: "Like Jodie Foster?"

—(Sn 5 Ep 5)

Judith Butler

"Let's see, *Gender Trouble*, Judith Butler, 📖 it should be here!"

—Paris (Sn 7 Ep 14)

Angela Bassett

Bassett has an impressive acting résumé, but it all started with her master's in fine arts from the Yale School of Drama (1983). I'm not sure how the Gilmores would feel about Bassett's most recent role as Queen Ramonda in the *Black Panther* series, but I do think Rory would have been a fan of Bassett's stage performance as Lady Macbeth 📖 (1998).

Lupita Nyong'o

Nyong'o also graduated from the Yale School of Drama and was cast as Nakia in the famous superhero series, *Black Panther*. Maybe we should look into a *Black Panther*/Yale connection here?

Bellamy Young

Initially at Yale to study physics, Young later switched her focus to a double major in English and theater. Clearly, that paid off as Young is well known for her role as Mellie on *Scandal*, a show that's one of the famous brainchildren of dynamite writer and producer Shonda Rhimes. Young also sang in Yale's a cappella group Mixed Company, something Richard Gilmore would approve of.

13

Singing Songs of Gemstones

The Power of Music

"Music is my life."

—Lane (Sn 3 Ep 10)

Get ready to "Walk Like an Egyptian," study the "Mona Lisa," and find yourself "Reflecting Light." It's time to delve into the distinctly Gilmore world of music. From the unforgettable opening scene in the pilot of Lorelai walking to The La's "There She Goes," to rocking out to "Time Bomb" with Hep Alien, to the atmospheric "Heavenly" strummings of Stars Hollow's troubadour, music is the heartbeat of the show. For many TV series, music is relegated to the background to provide ambiance or round out the experiential nature of television. *Gilmore Girls* is different; its music provides another layer of characterization and reveals music's motivational power.

Creator Amy Sherman-Palladino wanted more than just a unique sound; she wanted the music to embody the characters' personalities. While she certainly accomplished that vision, the music became a character of its own, weaving a "Tapestry" of magic and community throughout the show. But before we get into the power of music and its importance in our lives, I want to take a moment to sing nostalgic about *Gilmore Girls'* most iconic music moments.

The title sequence and the accompanying musical theme has turned "Where You Lead" into a beloved ballad that not only speaks to the musical quality of the show and highlights the characters but also has a story of its own. Amy was a long-time fan of Carole King and thought the original version of the song resonated with the folksy charm and the theme of ultimate dedication that Amy envisioned for the show. When the *Gilmore* production team couldn't come up with a song that felt as perfect, Amy reached out to King for permission to use her song for the show. In a magical stroke of good fortune, Carole King said yes. The discussion then moved to the mother-daughter aspect that was central to *Gilmore Girls* and how "Where You Lead" might be altered to reflect that. *Variety* reports that Carole King added a few mother-daughter tweaks to the lyrics and recorded the updated song in her own home with her daughter, Louise Goffin, singing the harmonies heard in the chorus. Could there be a more perfect way to set the tone for the show?

The iconic "la-las" are next in the Gilmore musical ensemble, consisting of the simple guitar strumming and harmonic vocals that often provide a beautiful backdrop for many scenes in *Gilmore Girls*. Once again, the story behind the la-las is just as magical as the effect it creates. Written and performed by Sam Phillips, the la-las were used during transitional scenes but specifically crafted per Amy's instructions. Amy wanted the score "to be the music inside of Lorelai's or Rory's heads—and not just Lorelai's or Rory's, but it was the music that they shared." I've never thought of it that way before, but it rings so true. It's one more detail that not only gives color and context clues into the titular mother-daughter bond but also pulls us into their special "Little Corner of the World."

Speaking of customized music, there is nothing more quintessentially Stars Hollow than having a musician play songs that reflect your life. Enter: the Stars Hollow Town Troubadour. In case you couldn't tell already, Amy Sherman-Palladino fosters a tremendous love of music, and when *Gilmore* was in the production stage, she approached one of her favorite musicians,

Grant-Lee Phillips, to play the Stars Hollow troubadour. Phillips, his guitar, and sometimes his harmonica entertain the town with covers of "Be True to Your School" by the Beach Boys and "Wake Me Up Before You Go-Go" by Wham!, but he also showcases his original songs, many of which you can find on Phillips's solo album or from his time in a band called Grant Lee Buffalo. (See the end of this chapter for more.) However, the troubadour provides more than background music. As previously mentioned, his songs often replicate the internal dialogue running through Lorelai's and Rory's heads at pivotal moments. For example, in season three, the troubadour strums out "Smile," which talks about having no regrets, just as Lorelai and Rory start to freak out because Rory is going off to college soon and they won't be together as much. The troubadour's song represents their mental dialogue, knowing they'll never regret spending time in each other's company, underscoring the mother-daughter relationship that is so integral to both of their characters, the core of who they are.

Through the la-las and the troubadour, the viewer gets a more intimate and comprehensive picture of Lorelai and Rory. Knowing a character's most intimate thoughts is something normal in the world of literature. (Many writers use third-person limited, where you're aware of one character's thoughts, or third-person omniscient, where you know everything about everyone.) Readers are accustomed to this all-knowing sense of characterization, but TV shows are different. Unless the show utilizes voice-overs to give you a peek inside a character's mind, the dialogue and the action are the only clues you have to get the full scope of someone's personality. *Gilmore Girls* uses music to add an extra, more intimate layer of personalization. The tone and rhythm of the la-las and the tone and lyrics of the troubadour's songs either reinforce Lorelai's and Rory's inner feelings that they've already expressed on the show or reveal a more profound emotion that perhaps they're afraid to discuss out loud or don't even realize they feel, giving us access to more information than what the characters themselves can give us.

Sometimes, it can be challenging to accurately describe the complexities of our thoughts and feelings. Luckily for us, and the Gilmores, sometimes music can do that instead. Music speaks a truth that we often can't describe in any other way.

When the Gilmores are not listening to music, they're talking about it. Lorelai reads *I'm with the Band* by Pamela Des Barres and *The Dirt: Confessions of the World's Most Notorious Rock Band* by Mötley Crüe, revealing her interest in rock music in addition to the folksy '80s tunes she's so fond of. Lane is a devotee of *The Mojo Collection: The Ultimate Music Companion* by Jim Irvin and continues her obsession with *The Velvet Underground and Nico* by Joe Harvard; she's devoted to experiencing ALL the music. Jess studies *We Owe You Nothing – Punk Planet: The Collected Interviews* edited by Daniel Sinker, which, no surprise, matches perfectly with his beatnik reading tendencies and personality. He also wants to read *Please Kill Me: The Uncensored Oral History of Punk* by Legs McNeil and Gillian McCain but can't until Rory finishes it first. The characters' continual learning and engagement with all things music speaks to the "all in" mentality, in terms of culture, that the show is famous for.

For the big finale in our musical retrospective, we have the one, the only, Hep Alien! In season three, when Lane discovers a love of playing the drums, she secretly joins a local band, making them play songs like "London Calling" as quietly as possible so Mrs. Kim doesn't hear. Though the band (Dave, Brian, and Zack) doesn't have an official name at first, they later become Hep Alien. When Dave goes off to college, Gil, played by real-life rocker Sebastian Bach, steps in as his replacement, simultaneously upping their average age but also adding an edge that the three young Connecticut Yankees currently lack. Balancing out the folksy town music and Lorelai's '80s classics that usually underscore the show, Hep Alien brings rock and roll to Stars Hollow. While their sweet spot is songs like "White Riot" and some of their originals like "Rebecca in the Morning," the band also manages to add their own spin to "Believe It or Not," "Hollaback Girl," and "Hava Nagila." And let's not forget this Zack original, "Ah ah ah oh oh oh oh oh." (Extra points if you sang that in your head when you read it!)

For Lane, music becomes a necessary extension of her personality. We know Lorelai and Rory pretty well, but they're also always allowed to be themselves, so what we see is who they really are. However, Lane often must hide who she is because of her mother's strict rules. Lane can't wear the clothes, date the boys, or attend the activities she likes. Listening to and later playing music are the only ways she can express her true self, the only way she can reveal parts of her personality that she usually has to hide under her bedroom floorboards.

After all, music is a part of our creation story; we are born of rhythm. As fetuses, we grow inside our mother, surrounded by the sounds of her body, of her beating heart. That rhythmic interior is one of the first things we know. There, we are safe. There, we are whole. There, we have not been tainted with all the tumultuous events of life. When we are born, we leave that place, never to return. Just imagine, for a moment, that you have no fear, cynicism, imposter syndrome, or trauma; that if you knew that whatever you did, you'd be OK; that someone always had your back. What could you do if you felt like that? What would you be capable of if there was nothing to restrain you? That's the kind of environment we begin with, but its protection evaporates the second we are born. Can that feeling ever be recreated? Can we ever come close to the strength and power that lie in such complete wholeness?

In the few weeks I spent rereading *The Return of the King* and Nick Hornby's *Songbook*, I kept my eye out for any other musical revelations. However, in a stroke of staggering weirdness, it was *Brave*

New World by Aldous Huxley that supplied a perfect musical example. The dystopian novel, one I picture Jess really enjoying, depicts a universe so intentionally different from ours that concepts like "parents" and "marriage" are entirely archaic. In this world, everything is predestined: your place in society, your job, your friends, your hobbies–they even construct your beliefs.

But amid such a foreign climate, there was that one thing: rhythm. In the book, specific phrases are repeated to children while they sleep so that they internalize those messages, and as adults, those ideas become not just a part of their belief system but a method of grounding and calming. What do they do when they gather to celebrate their founder and their way of life? Clink their test tubes? No. They sing. Song after song, they extol the virtues of their leader, just like singing Christmas carols in church, and somewhat reminiscent of the people of Gondor welcoming Aragorn in *The Return of the King*. Music is everywhere, even where you least suspect it.

Aside from entertainment, my first instinct is to use music to be calming and grounding. Like Lorelai and Rory separately blast Macy Gray's "I Try" in the pilot episode after they fight, I use music to regulate my emotions. As a child, lullabies eased me into sleep, and Christmas carols still lower my cortisol levels as an adult; these melodies pull all the fine threads of energy flowing out of me into a tight braid, organized and controlled but strong and centered.

I read a quote earlier this year that said, "Rest is where you become more you." But I'd like to amend that to say music is where you become more you. From the very beginning, the melody of our heart beating and the chorus of our blood pumping has instilled within us a need for this rhythm. Whether we find it playing the radio, moving back and forth in a rocking chair, dancing at a club, or swaying our hands back and forth as we walk, we have that rhythm in our lives. And we need it to fortify and sustain us. But do we always unlock music's full potential?

Looking back, there was one time in my life when, like Lane, music was the one thing that kept me going. In 2013, I ran the Chicago Marathon.

I had tread hundreds of miles on the Chicago streets, weaving my way around the city, training for over a year. When I wasn't running, I researched. I read all the articles about persevering when it came to "hitting the wall": the dreaded twentieth mile where your body and mind threaten to give up entirely. There's only so much training one can do for the unimaginable, but I was going to do my best to prepare anyway.

For weeks, I had dedicated time to compiling a running playlist. I accessed every song that ever resonated with me for its ability to invoke the strength I would need to keep going. However, the final song, which I planned to play on the hill that led to the finish line, was one of the most crucial aspects of my preparation. That tune had to be so powerful as to make my mind and body forget that every muscle was screaming in pain and to make me continue onward despite everything that held me back.

Is there even such a power? I believe there is: music. The rhythm. The beat. "You Can't Stop the Beat" is what the final song in the musical *Hairspray* says. And I agree. Experts will tell you that a certain number of beats per minute is optimal for running. It makes sense, but was I going to look up all the bpms for each song on my playlist? No. All I needed was for the song to be so strong and instantaneously invigorating that it needed to feel like I had donned a ring of power. And "You Can't Stop the Beat" did it for me. The tempo of that song propelled me forward, reverberating in my body each time my foot struck the pavement, pushing my legs onward despite all ills, driving my heart to keep circulating blood and oxygen through my body, shaping me into a being that knew only one thing: the beat.

It's that all-encompassing feature of music that holds its power. It brings together every shaft of light within you until it forms a beam so concentrated it incinerates all that stands in its path. That is the power of music. It strings together all the emotions, all the thoughts and notes of every story we've ever been a part of. It's a lifeline, a tremendous power for those who embrace it.

It's now our task to find music again—not just the obvious music, like turning on Spotify more or the radio, but our natural rhythms and where they harmonize with the notes of the world around us. Everything has its own frequency—extraordinary in its individuality but also as a part of the whole. Remember that sometimes the grandest overtures are in the smallest of things: the soft scrape of a page-turning, the vibrations in your legs as you walk through town, the hushed chorus of falling snow, and the steadfast beat of your heart, because those are the individual instruments that make up the orchestra.

So next time you're not feeling like yourself or you can't express what you're feeling, when the path ahead seems too treacherous to traverse, or when you need to calm down, ask yourself, "What is my Hep Alien? What tune would my official troubadour play right now? What music makes me dance in the car like Lorelai does to 'Shadow Dancing,' her favorite song from high school? What makes my heart sing like Rory unpacking a new box of books? How can I incorporate more music into my life to keep me going no matter the odds?" All you have to do is turn on some music like Lane, Lorelai, and Rory and reconnect to the rhythms that sing in each of our souls.

Turn up the music, Gilmore.

Top Songs from the Stars Hollow Town Troubadour

- "Heavenly"—Grant-Lee Phillips
- "Everybody Needs a Little Sanctuary"—Grant Lee Buffalo
- "Jubilee"—Grant Lee Buffalo
- "Be True to Your School"—The Beach Boys
- "Wake Me Up Before You Go-Go"—Wham!
- "Mona Lisa"—Grant-Lee Phillips
- "Lily-A-Passion"—Grant-Lee Phillips

- "Mama Tried"–Merle Haggard
- Hear all of the Town Troubadour's songs here:

Wherefore Art Thou Hep Alien

Every band needs a cool name, but Lane, Zack, Brian, and Dave have trouble coming up with one. Brian suggests The Harry Potters, 📖 and Zack is a fan of Follow Them to the Edge of the Desert, quite the lengthy moniker. While we don't get to see how the band came up with the name on the show, we do know the real-life story: Amy Sherman-Palladino rearranged the letters in one of her producers' names. That producer? Helen Pai. Thus, Hep Alien was born.

Where to Listen to Gilmore Playlists

- WB Spotify Playlist:

- Gilmore Fan-Made Playlist:

- Fan-Made Playlist:

- Sam Phillips:

- Carole King:

- The Bangles:

- Grant-Lee Phillips:

- Hep Alien Fan-Made Playlist:

14

Not Better in Philadelphia

Discussing the Intricacies of Health and Wellness

"Pain is part of life."

—Richard (Sn 1 Ep 10)

There's a soothing level of certainty in *Gilmore Girls*, an assurance that no matter what, the little bubble of Stars Hollow and its residents will remain relatively untouched by the ravages of life. No one is freezing to death *Little Match Girl*–style or facing horrific, life-threatening challenges like those in *The Bielski Brothers.* In the Gilmores' world, reality has less influence: the termites will be handled, and money problems will be solved. Healthwise, they can eat whatever they want, including all the junk food one can think of, and not have to worry about gaining weight, getting diabetes, or rotting their teeth. They don't even have to exercise other than walking around the town because somehow, calories don't exist! Chronic illnesses and disabilities are completely absent too; they show up only when there's a function and a cause for Emily and Richard to support.

Yes, the Gilmores somehow have access to the fountain of health and are spared some of the world's harsher realities. There is, however, an exception to this: Richard's heart attacks.

Before we get into this discussion, I want to mention that we're going to delve into some challenging subjects here: illness, death, mental health, and the discomfort of discussing health-related matters. If reading this chapter is a bit much for you right now, please move on to another section of this book and return when you feel ready. You're welcome to do this with any of the chapters, but I find discussing and holding space for medical ordeals can be particularly traumatic. So, proceed with self-awareness and grace.

Richard's first medical episode, revealed to be angina, comes as a surprise during the Gilmores' annual Christmas dinner. Richard goes to adjust the thermostat during dinner, and disaster strikes. The scene immediately cuts to Lorelai in Luke's diner and the famous Santa Burger, so we don't see Richard collapse or being rushed to the hospital; we are privy only to the aftermath, and only from Lorelai's point of view.

Usually, Lorelai's the one with all the energy and action plans, but when she hears about her father, her brain turns to mush. Even when she arrives at the hospital, it's difficult for her to go into Richard's room, and she keeps inventing reasons to avoid seeing him.

Emily, on the other hand, is all about setting things in order. She's found some good pillows and slippers and made sure Richard has his choice of newspapers when he wakes up. She puts on the appearance of handling things, but it's not until Richard broaches the subject of his will that Emily begins to break down. And in a heartbreaking gesture, she demands that Richard cannot die before she does; she demands to go first. Her love for Richard and her fear of losing him completely overwhelm her.

In contrast to Lorelai and Emily, Rory's reaction is relatively modest. She's unsure how to act, telling Lorelai she feels she should be doing something. This is Rory's first encounter with something as serious as a heart attack, so her hesitations are understandable.

Then there's Luke. From the minute Lorelai gets the call about Richard, Luke is all in. He drives Lorelai to the hospital, checks in on Rory and her feelings, and even comforts Emily when she explains her attachment to Richard's bow tie. Luke is the rock in this scenario, providing comfort and reassurance to each of the Gilmore girls in turn and helping out when needed. Though Lorelai and Rory momentarily discuss Rory's feelings about the whole thing, it's Luke who checks in with each Gilmore and shares a touching moment with them individually.

Since all of this takes place in season one, this is the first time we're experiencing a true crisis with the Gilmores. The viewer is accustomed to the characters' daily mannerisms and reactions at this point, but this medical emergency allows us to get a different perspective of Lorelai, Rory, Emily, and Richard. *Gilmore Girls*, while containing some low-stakes dramatic elements, is a comedy, and the comedic moments allow these characters to shine. However, in order for these characters to be believable, they have to experience a certain level of reality.

There is no right way to process a medical emergency. While the reactions of others may not always resonate with what we're feeling, they're all valid (minus being completely absent like Christopher in season seven). As Lorelai reflects after the Independence Inn catches on fire in season three, you might imagine what it would be like when an unexpected tragedy strikes, but you never know for sure until you experience it. All you can do is respond with love.

The seventh season of *Gilmore Girls* depicts Richard's second health scare. He is now teaching an economics course at Yale, which Rory is attending, and he experiences pain in his arm and collapses at the start of the class.

Lorelai rushes to the hospital, waiting with Rory to talk to the doctor and calling Emily and Christopher. Her hesitancy in engaging with her father from his first episode has receded, and she tries to make Richard smile, reassures him that he still looks good, and babbles about the pros and cons of being in Philadelphia. Rory's timidity has disappeared too. She accompanies Richard to the emergency room, is more open with her feelings, and is more present in the moment when comforting Richard. Undoubtedly, both Rory and Lorelai have learned a little something since Richard's first hospitalization.

Emily, however, has another classic Emily freakout, criticizing everyone from the staff at their country club to the nurses at the hospital. She regains her composure once they're allowed to see Richard before his surgery and promptly goes into action mode again: contacting their lawyer to update their legal papers, stocking up on every type of fish imaginable for their omega-3s, and rearranging their schedules and staff at their home.

The Gilmore guys are at entirely different ends of the spectrum here. Logan helicopters in and puts off business meetings to keep Rory company and help get Emily's fish delivery squared away. Luke drives straight to the hospital to offer his well-wishes and help; Emily sends him to get Richard's car, and of course, Luke returns later with bags of food. Christopher, however, is totally MIA, not responding to Lorelai's multiple calls. When he finally does show up, he spends only the bare minimum of time with his family and does nothing to help or comfort anyone. I know he and Lorelai are fighting at the time, but come on, Christopher. When there's a family emergency, it's all hands on deck.

With the surprise of Richard's first heart problems, you'd think the Gilmores would be a little more concerned about health. Do they start going to the doctor for regular checkups? Does Lorelai have a health care directive and a will so Rory will know what to do? What kind of health practices is she teaching Rory anyway? In season five, Lorelai has to call and check that Rory is using protection while having sex, so one could infer that *if* they've had this conversation before, it wasn't very thorough. Lorelai, Rory, and sometimes Emily go right back to how things were before without considering any of these medical issues. Perhaps their actions would have been different if they had discussed some of these problems.

If the Gilmores are inexperienced with caring for their physical health, they seem to struggle even more with their mental health. They see therapy as something only for "people who lick parking meters"; Emily rejects it after Richard's first heart attack and his retirement, it's seen as a joke when Yale requires Rory to attend a few therapy sessions before returning to school, and it's only a one-off when Lorelai talks to Lynnie in the car about Luke. Mental health books don't appear on Rory's reading list, either, so she's not engaging with any helpful information in that way. Self-care may not have been the big issue then as it is today, but it's certainly missing from their lives.

We may not all eat a Gilmorean amount of sugar every day, but for some, including the Gilmores, there is a sense of trust that your health will always be fine. I was way too young—thirteen—when I learned how precarious my health could be, and I know others have had similar experiences. Since then, I've discovered that talking about health makes it easier and less scary to encounter. None of these are fun topics for discussion, but they're worthwhile conversations to have with people you consider family. You never know when life is going to throw you a curve ball, and you'll have to learn to adjust, like learning *How to Breathe Underwater*.

Looking back, I think my initial health and sex education was pretty standard. We had health class in school, and my mom, and a few young adult health books, supplemented additional information when needed. You don't need to have end-of-life care talks with toddlers or anything, but I believe we should discuss all health topics in proportion to one's age and situation. It should also be something that friends talk about (you know, in addition to the big game or the essay they have to write for their homework), because sometimes talking about health issues with your peers is easier.

In middle school, when I first noticed pain in my legs that eventually spread throughout my body, I got a crash course in what it means to deal with health. Suddenly, my life involved X-rays, blood tests, symptom journals, pills, and injections, in addition to studying and attending school.

But simply having the experience doesn't make talking about it any easier. Unfortunately, you do have to practice that part. I remember I could barely get the words out to tell one of my friends just how sick I was, and my mom had to come in and help me explain. For years, I told only my closest friends and family, guarding my secret like contraband books in *Fahrenheit 451* or *1984*. Even when I did discuss my illness with a chosen few, the conversations were awkward, and I often wished I had prepared what I was going to say beforehand.

When I first experienced symptoms, the two cousins we saw the most were toddlers. I had an extremely difficult time trying to communicate with them. They wanted to run around and play, anything that required energy, and I had issues summoning enough strength to sit in a chair. My illness was problematic enough to discuss with adults, who at least had a frame of reference for medical issues and the aches of having a body that's growing older. How was I supposed to articulate the details of chronic disease to a pair of kids, or even to my friends, who had boundless energy and knew nothing of never-ending pain? How do you explain something to someone who can't understand what you're going through?

Just as Odin traded his eye for the key to unlocking the mysteries of the universe and as Rory's break from Yale and her mother forced her to evaluate her life, pain can be the price of wisdom. Unfortunately, there are some things, like a prolonged illness, that you just can't understand until you've felt them. Pain has an immense power to push you past your breaking point, to force you beyond the body, the mind, and the being that you were, to shove you into a world where you know nothing but must adapt to survive. Until you've fought your way through that gauntlet, that visceral knowledge isn't part of your body yet. That's not your fault, and no one would wish such misfortune on you in order to understand their experience. You can still offer comfort in many ways, but it does create a knowledge gap that is often difficult to traverse and can inadvertently cause a greater distance between you and your community.

The blueprint for my journey in discussing health starts with Miss Patty and one of her little quips that are often too mature for her audience.

In one dance class, Patty's students walk around with books on their heads to improve their posture. She tells them to "walk smooth. That's a new *Harry Potter* on your heads. If they should drop, Harry will die, and there won't be any more books" (Sn 1 Ep 2). If there weren't any more Harry Potter books like Miss Patty had threatened, I would not have been inspired to change how I was thinking and talking about my health.

Alastor Moody, or Mad-Eye Moody as he is more commonly known in *Harry Potter*, is a dark wizard catcher with extensive knowledge about the darkness that can ensnare a witch or wizard. When we meet him in *Harry Potter and the Goblet of Fire,* we learn he lost his leg and eye in battles against evil. While he walks on a prosthetic leg, his lost eye is supplanted by a magical one that can see through the back of his head and invisibility cloaks. His biggest physical tragedy brought him one of his most powerful abilities, a magical power almost no one else possesses.

Seeing beyond what's in front of you is a rare power, even in the magical world. Pop culture is full of examples of those who transform their trauma into their superpower. Lorelai turns the loss of her home into extreme creativity, turning what could have been an Oliver Twist–ian childhood for Rory into a Wonka-esque fun land where everything had the potential for entertainment. A neurologist would describe this as forging new neural pathways, which increases the workings in your brain, allowing you to continue to push further and further, creating new passageways. This is how your mind changes, how your wisdom expands, how, like Moody and Lorelai, you learn to see invisible things.

It's easy to imagine seeing invisible objects and having mind-reading abilities in books about magic, but in the real world, seeing invisible things is an ability acquired only through extreme circumstances and hard work, like enduring excruciating pain for prolonged periods of time. Many chronic illnesses are called invisible illnesses for a reason: you cannot physically see something wrong as you can with a broken leg or chicken pox. Because of my experience with chronic illness, I've been able to train the part of my brain that sees invisible things in others, honing a superpower of my own. When some people see someone who is shy or not taking part in a social gathering, I see traces of exhaustion, anxiety, emotional upheaval, or more. I'm not saying I assign all these assumed emotions to someone; rather, I'm looking for the story behind what my eyes don't immediately see. Just like readers must read between the lines, I've learned to read between the lines of humanity, gaining insights that aren't outwardly projected.

If *Gilmore Girls* and *Harry Potter* could show me how to use my trauma to develop a new way of looking at things, could it also help me feel more comfortable with sharing my story? The more I studied works of literature and television, the more I saw fragments of plot and dialogue that also described my experience, aiding me in crafting pop culture analogies like similes and metaphors to bring understanding to a subject shrouded in unknowns. Later, for example, when my cousins had seen some of the *Harry Potter* movies, I could have told them that my body was like Voldemort after his first downfall, weak and unable to do anything. I could have told them that because of my pain, I was now like Moody: I had lost parts of myself to my illness and may never get them back, but I gained new powers of observation, almost as if I could see what was invisible. The worlds of literature, TV, and movies have an unlimited supply of parallels to draw from—part of the reason I'm so passionate about helping people use these mediums to understand and transform their lives.

Now, when I'm at a loss for what to say, I flip through my pop culture repertoire to help me out. A friend's parent is in the hospital? I'll be your Luke, get you where you need to go, bring food, and be there for moral support. Experiencing issues with your mental health? I've got Paris's whiteboard and markers, ready to tackle the tasks that feel daunting to you. If you're feeling lost in life? I have Jess's "WHY DID YOU DROP OUT OF YALE?" speech queued up to help you reconnect with what's essential to you.

To replicate this analogy theory for yourself, think of a moment in the show with a feeling similar to what you're going through and try to imagine what that character might say or do. Need to enforce some boundaries? Imagine Lorelai moving out of her parents' house to get her own space (but I'd also add that you don't want to have the troubled relationship Lorelai has with her parents, so ensure you're setting up these boundaries to prevent that). Use the situation, feelings, and even character dialogue to help you craft a metaphor that applies to your situation. This will help you begin a genuine and honest dialogue with others.

I consider my health journey akin to what Lorelai and Rory's Yale Graduation Celebration Trip would have been, one roller coaster after another. But in learning to use the Gilmores' lives and other examples from pop culture as metaphors for my own, I've been able to open up more and ask for what I need and if I don't know, then to try different methods until I find what's suitable for me.

All of our mind-bodies are different. They'll have different requirements and quirks, and even those change over time. The critical part is getting to know what your health needs are. I've discovered this is often a process of trial and error to find—or say—the right thing, but what matters is that you're trying. Clearly, eating all that fish wasn't satisfactory for Richard, but thankfully, Sookie could step in and make some of her healthy *and* tasty meals for him. Consult your doctors, get a different doctor if you need to, do your research, and test things out.

You know your body best; you're the expert. Once you find what works, commit to that and communicate with those around you, but respectfully, don't make five-star chefs so miserable that they quit your service. Put those powerful pop culture metaphors to work for you!

As Richard learns with his second heart attack and surgery, all those other problems, goals, and ideas take a back seat when your health is disrupted. Those disturbances tend to emphasize certain things in your life, like how precious and how precarious our health can be. But hopefully, with me and the Gilmores on your team, you feel empowered to take charge of your own health habits and how to discuss what really matters to you with those who care about you.

If you're going through a health battle when you read this book or encounter one somewhere down the road, I want you to know you're not alone. No matter how you feel right now or how your friends and family are reacting, you'll always have this case file of Gilmore health experiences to turn to for comfort, inspiration, direction, and hope.

Take care of yourself, Gilmore.

I Am an Autumn: A Tribute to the Gilmores We've Lost

Edward Herrmann – Richard Gilmore

With Edward Herrmann's passing in 2014, a beloved part of the *Gilmore Girls* magic vanished forever. His loss is made even more devastating by the depiction of his character's two heart attacks on the show, a gut-wrenching foreshadowing of the health issues that would eventually take away a prominent figure not just on *Gilmore Girls* but in the acting world and in the hearts of many fans, friends, and family. Just as Trix's original obituary didn't do her justice, these paragraphs cannot hold the entirety of the genius that was Ed Herrmann. From his depiction of FDR in *Annie* to his guest appearances on shows like *Law & Order, How I Met Your Mother*, and *Grey's Anatomy,* to even lending his vocal talents to documentaries, Ed brought his heart and soul into everything he did.

Edward and his beloved portrayal of Richard Gilmore will always maintain a place in our hearts, just as if there were a massive portrait of Richard hanging on a wall nearby. Though we'll miss the person and actor he was, we'll always be able to return to *Gilmore Girls* for another rewatch to cherish the memories we have of him.

Brian Tarantina – Bootsy

It doesn't matter whether they appear once or many times in the series; each member of Stars Hollow is still treasured. Brian played Bootsy on *Gilmore Girls,* the owner of the town's magazine stand, but he also has an extensive history in other popular movies and TV shows, including his stint as the Gaslight emcee on *The Marvelous Mrs. Maisel.* Brian unexpectedly passed away in 2019, leaving a Bootsy-shaped hole in all of our hearts. In the glorious words of Rachel Brosnahan's Instagram post, "Our family of weirds won't be the same without him."

Everyone has their weird qualities, but finding a superb group of weirdos that make your kookiness feel normal is what makes a beautiful family. I've found a beautiful, weird family in the Gilmore fandom, and it just won't be the same without Edward Herrmann and Brian Tarantina.

We miss you, Gilmore.

But We're Skint

The Complexities of Money and Gratitude

"I'm not going to be on the *Fortune* 500 list anytime soon, but I'm fine."

—Lorelai (Sn 4 Ep 12)

Money, money, money, must be funny in a Gilmore's world. Starting with the pilot, when Lorelai borrows money from Emily and Richard to pay for Chilton, money is introduced as a major theme in the series. Finances not only are repeatedly mentioned but also cause some of the biggest upheavals in the Gilmore family, establishing money as the bedrock of the Gilmore environment from the very beginning.

In the dichotomy between the haves and the have-nots, Richard and Emily Gilmore were born and raised in silver-spoon households. Ivy League educations, trust funds, and staying at the Ritz in Paris were a given—and so on and so forth for all the generations to come.

The expectation of the abundance of money underlies their entire world. The same goes for Logan Huntzberger, whose privileged antics are straight out of *Less Than Zero*. But this *Extravagance* comes with expectations, too, a VIP kind of lifestyle, associations with the "right" (a.k.a. monied) people, and a respectable household. One does not spit out the silver spoon unless you're Pop-Tart–loving Lorelai Gilmore.

Lorelai was always uncomfortable with the trappings of her parents' world. They wanted poufy dresses with crinoline skirts, and Lorelai wanted to wear sneakers. They turned up their noses at packaged foods, and Lorelai thought Pop-Tarts tasted like "freedom and rebellion and independence." And then, Lorelai got pregnant. Both sets of parents decided that Lorelai and Christopher, the baby daddy, should get married, but Lorelai had other ideas. So, she packed up what little she had and moved out. She had no money, no job, and nowhere to live.

Landing in Stars Hollow was a blessing for Lorelai. Mia, the owner of the Independence Inn, gave Lorelai a job as a maid and allowed Lorelai and Rory to live in an old toolshed on the grounds. Finally, Lorelai had found a life where she was in control of how she wanted to live, but that life came with drawbacks, specifically a major lack of money.

Though Lorelai and Rory live in a beautiful home when we first meet them and have all the take-out food, books, and book covers they want, there are still physical traces and stories from the time when Lorelai was broke. We know Lorelai's bed was an old one from the Independence Inn, that Lorelai saved up for a long time to buy her couch, and that her talent for sewing came from the time when she had to turn her own clothes into baby outfits for Rory.

For the most part, Stars Hollow is on equal monetary status with Lorelai and Rory, with two notable exceptions. Luke, who is a bachelor who never spends money on anything, has enough savings to give Lorelai a considerable loan when she buys the Dragonfly Inn and has recouped enough to later buy the biggest home in town, the Twickham House. Then we have Kirk, who later reveals he has a quarter of a million dollars in his bid against Luke for the Twickham House. Luke and Kirk are notable exceptions to the Stars Hollow economy; the rest of the residents consider themselves to be wealthy in terms of companionship, laughter, and love.

My first recollection of worrying about money was in my sophomore year of high school and originated from one thing: medical bills. While I never saw the details of the bills, I knew they frequently came in the mail, and it was all because of me. My parents insisted that my health was the number one priority and that whatever treatment I required, they'd find a way to pay for it. That kind of devotion brings tears to my eyes and an understanding of just how lucky I was and am to be able to afford medical care like that. Knowing that my existence required more money to be spent in my name than the rest of my family combined is a weight I've harbored for years and has continually informed my relationship with money, just like Lorelai's early childhood informed hers.

It wasn't until after I graduated and moved to LA, though, that the reality of money really slapped me in the face. Remember when Lane moves into her first apartment and is shocked to find that there isn't even a refrigerator and all they have is three stereos and no towels? I had a similar experience in my new apartment (but I at least had towels). I had no furniture or household appliances—big or small. At the time, I worked two jobs: one in retail at the mall and one unpaid internship at a digital magazine, so money was very tight.

I knew two people when I moved to LA, and I didn't even know them that well; they were my dad's cousin and her husband. She gave me all kinds of hand-me-downs from their house—pots and pans, dishes, even an old DVD player, which I used to watch and rewatch the first three seasons of *Gilmore Girls* that I found in the $5 bin at a bargain store. I'd sit on the blow-up mattress (later replaced by a futon) in that empty apartment, my cat and the Gilmores my only company and entertainment.

I was fully aware of how much this situation resembled Mia giving Lorelai old furniture and home items from the Independence Inn to get her started. Without that kindness, we'd both have been without the essentials of a home, a safety net I'm grateful to have had then and now.

Whenever I'm unable to buy the things or experiences I want because of money, I think of my health, the empty LA apartment, and my current NY home, remembering I'm fortunate enough to have the basics. I may not always have what I want, but I have what I need.

Shakespeare said, "Neither a borrower nor a lender be." Clearly, the Gilmores don't subscribe to that ideal because loaning money is a pivotal part of the first episode and a cornerstone of the rest of the series. Therefore, we need to carefully weigh all the money advice we read or see on TV to see whether it applies to our lives. I don't know who's reading this right now, but I'm going to guess that most of you are not in the "Emily Gilmore buys a private plane" financial bracket, so I'm going to focus on some of the more relatable fiduciary scenarios in *Gilmore Girls*. Please keep in mind that though I may have read *A Monetary History of the United States* by Milton Friedman and Anna Schwartz, I am not a financial advisor, just a person reading way too much into *Gilmore Girls*.

First up, let's talk about earning money. As soon as Lorelai moves out, she gets a job as a maid at the Independence Inn and works her way up. She saves a lot of money by living on the property, thus earning enough to eventually buy her beloved house. Saving up in any way you can to achieve your big goals? Seems like a solid financial plan to me.

As hardworking as Lorelai is, this trait doesn't seem to rub off on Rory, and Lorelai doesn't enforce it. I understand that school is Rory's priority, and I felt the same when I was in school (which is why I had a part-time retail job so I could proudly buy my own Pop-Tarts), but when Rory's in college, she rarely gets or retains a part-time job or saves what she earns. Her cafeteria card swiping lasts only one episode. After that, she does a week-long stint taking inventory at Stars Hollow Books, though she ends up buying more books, practically erasing anything she's earned. Minus the DAR job that she takes when she's not at school, that's it until she graduates. We know Rory's tuition is covered by the Gilmores, but is Lorelai still paying for everything? Books? Food? Clothes? Gas? It seems so strange to me that Lorelai would be OK with this, considering her background.

Lorelai is so stingy when it comes to taking money from her parents, but it's totally OK for her to pay for everything for Rory even when Rory is living on her own? Seems like a double standard to me.

Our beloved Gilmores make mistakes, but the silver lining is that we get to learn from their errors. I think the lesson here is to work when you can–not to an obsessive extent à la Kirk, though he ends up with a lot of money for all the sitting around at Luke's that he does. (Maybe he invests on the side?) You never know what life is going to throw at you. Paris found this out the hard way when her parents went bankrupt in season six and she had to get a job for the first time in her life as a waitress for Rory's DAR party. It helps to have money to afford to pay bills or unexpected expenses or tide you over between jobs. And when you do have money, spend it wisely. That brings us to one of the most controversial Gilmore lifestyle practices tied to finances: eating out.

The Lorelai and Rory we first meet in the pilot season are basically the queens of takeout. They eat at Luke's every day, plus they order pizza and Chinese often. While the food there has small-town prices, and they're good about eating the leftovers, it still seems hazy as a responsible monetary practice. Even Richard mentions the senselessness of this Gilmore habit during his visit to Stars Hollow. I'm by no means a person who cooks (my version of dinner is usually eggs or yogurt), but I still try to eat in way more than I eat out. If I don't feel like cooking, there are plenty of freezer meals that are cheaper than getting takeaway.

Lorelai and Rory also spend money in other ways. They love shopping, they talk about getting mani-pedis, and Rory's endlessly buying books (seriously, girl, go to the library and get those free books!). However, talking to the fans and a little internet search will reveal that the biggest lifestyle red flag is Lorelai and Rory's habit of eating out for almost every single meal. Even if they're not tipping Luke (you don't have to tip the proprietor of an establishment), that still adds up to a lot of money over time.

While proper money management is important, gratitude is also a must when it comes to discussing finances. It's the drastic comparison of the lack of funds with the safety that money can bring that informed Lorelai's gratitude and inspires mine. She knew what it was like to have everything, but she also knew what it was like to have nothing. As she slowly worked to buy a real home for her and Rory, Lorelai was able to feel that gratitude firsthand. I believe it's one of the reasons she loves her house so much—she worked so hard for it and remembers the time when she had no home. Lorelai's house became the visual manifestation of her hard work and how far she's come.

Gratitude isn't always easy, and reminding oneself to practice it can be a lifelong challenge. When I forget, there are always books like *Oliver Twist,* *The Jungle*, and many more to put my situation in perspective. Being thankful is an essential part of appreciating what I have, and if most books and articles on happiness are to be believed, gratitude is a part of being truly happy.

However, budgeting like your life depends on it because your life *does* depend on it is a poor recipe for happiness. It can feel as if you're holding up the world on your back. This is how I felt over the past year when I left my steady job and paycheck to pursue writing. I had some savings to cover expenses for a while, but things got truly "Lorelai sitting in a dark room because she was going broke refurbishing the Dragonfly Inn" at one point. Since I'm a writer, you might call it the "starving artist" phase. I was never starving, for which I'm very thankful, but I was on a strict *Nickel and Dimed*–type budget. Bye-bye to subscriptions and eating out, so long to any paid entertainment, adios to vacations, new clothes, and so much more. It was a stressful sacrifice but one I knew I had to make.

Lorelai's creativity has definitely influenced me during this phase. While I can't make entire dresses like Lorelai, I can sew enough to patch a hole in some of my clothes. I've repaired my nightstand a few times, and even though the back of it has entirely come off and the door hinge is a total goner, I've accepted it, just as Lorelai accepted that her back door lock doesn't work and the porch light is out. I walk in the park for exercise like Lorelai and Rory walk around Stars Hollow. I look out for free park performances instead of going to the theater, almost like Lorelai and

Rory listening to the wedding music from the Independence Inn as their evening entertainment. And yes, just like Lorelai, I use coupons—don't ever let a Rory shame you over coupons! Most people have some kind of creativity inside them already, but I do believe that life also has a way of forcing creativity out of you. And I don't mean papier-mâché; I mean the "make it work" Tim Gunn kind of creativity.

No one's going to be buying any Birkin bags after reading this essay (I'm certainly not), but hopefully this chapter gave you something to think about. Maybe some reinforcements to bolster you while you're saving up for a big purchase, or maybe it encouraged you to start an emergency fund (we're talking a fund larger than Paris's green tea stash, here). Maybe it reminded you to look for moments of gratitude during your day or inspired you to be a little creative regarding your money. And remember, wealth can be found in many places: in the smiles of a friend, a hug from your chosen family, and the love of a community as dedicated as the Gilmores.

Spend responsibly, Gilmore.

And speaking of Birkin bags . . .

A Brief History of the Birkin Bag

When Rory lives with her grandparents, Emily and Richard snoop through the pool house to gain information about Rory's life. They don't find CIA documents in her purse, but Emily does spy the coveted Hermès Birkin bag, a gift from Logan.

Costumer Valerie Campbell confirms on TikTok that, yes, they used a real Birkin bag on *Gilmore Girls*. It was kept under lock and key, and a producer escorted the bag to set every time it was needed. But where is the bag today? Only the props team knows!

Emily Gilmore is obsessed with the Birkin bag, and frankly, so is the rest of the world. In 1984, Jane Birkin, a British actress, was on a flight to London. Jean-Louis Dumas, the executive chairman of luxury brand Hermès, listened to Birkin's wish for a fashionable bag that would fit everything she had to carry as a mother. With a rectangular shape that was spacious enough to hold one's belongings, gorgeous leather, classic details, and a dedicated space to hold a baby bottle, the Birkin bag was born.

But it didn't have the cult status then that it does now. It wasn't until the 1990s that the Birkin gained popularity, even being mentioned in 2002's *Sex and the City*, 🎬 a show that several brands can thank for their boost in popularity. (Sarah Jessica Parker has since confirmed to *Vogue* that they used a fake Birkin on the show.)

An Original Recipe from Larisa Kliman, Creator of *Eating Gilmore*, Inspired by Luke's Diner

Cooking meals at home is a great way to save money, and now you can enjoy one of Luke's iconic breakfasts by using ingredients you probably already have in your kitchen. Enjoy!

PUMPKIN PANCAKES

INGREDIENTS:

For the pancakes:

½ cup pumpkin puree

1¼ cup milk

2 eggs

2 tbsp granulated sugar

½ tsp vanilla

3 tbsp melted butter

1¾ cup all-purpose flour

¼ tsp salt

1 tbsp baking powder

1 tsp pumpkin pie spice (if you don't have pumpkin pie spice, you can also use allspice or a combination of cinnamon, nutmeg, and ground ginger)

¼ tsp ground cloves

For the cinnamon butter:

1 cup heavy cream

1⁄2 tbsp cinnamon

2 tsp brown sugar

DIRECTIONS:

1. In a large bowl, mix together the pumpkin, milk, eggs, sugar, vanilla, and melted butter until fully combined.
2. Mix in the flour, salt, baking powder, and spices. Stir together until fully combined. Some lumps are OK.
3. Turn on an electric griddle to 300°F or place a large skillet over medium heat.
4. Melt a teaspoon of butter or canola oil so the pancakes don't stick.
5. Pour about ¼ cup of the pancake batter onto your cooking surface. You can work in batches or one at a time, depending on the size of your skillet or griddle.
6. Allow the pancake to cook for about 2-3 minutes on each side. When small bubbles have formed on the uncooked side, it's time to flip the pancake.
7. While you're cooking the rest of the pancakes, keep the finished ones warmed under foil or in the oven set to the warming setting.
8. To make the cinnamon butter, add the heavy cream to a large mixing bowl. Using an electric mixer with the whisk attachment, whisk the cream for about 10-15 minutes on the highest setting.

9. The cream will first turn to whipped cream and then will begin to solidify. Liquid will separate out from the solids. This is buttermilk, don't discard it! (You can use it for other recipes!) Once the solids have turned yellow and have started to form together, stop mixing.
10. Strain the butter from the buttermilk with a fine mesh sieve. Then squeeze the butter to remove more of the buttermilk.
11. Run the butter under cold water for about 15 seconds, then squeeze out the liquid again.
12. Transfer the butter to a small mixing bowl and add the cinnamon and brown sugar. Stir to combine fully.

16

Thanks for the Monogrammed Towels

On the Parenting Styles That Shape Us

"I do all of this so you don't get hurt."

—Mrs. Kim (Sn 2 Ep 13)

Gilmore Girls gives us a delectable smorgasbord of parenting styles—from Lorelai and Emily to Luke, Liz, Sherry, Mrs. Kim, and Christopher, we're treated to every color in the parenting rainbow, allowing us to find comfort, laughter, and lessons in the various parental situations and figures. We all know that our biological parents and those who raise us directly impact the person we become, but what about all the other parents in our lives? What about our TV parents?

The mother-daughter relationship between Rory and Lorelai (and Emily and Lorelai) forms the foundation and main attraction of the show. But don't worry; this isn't a repeat of chapter 1. Instead, we will take a closer look at the relationships we haven't already discussed and the effects of different parenting styles.

Parenting decisions have equal potential for triumphs and missteps because, hello, parents are human, and as Rory points out in season seven, they make mistakes too. This means when discussing parenting in this chapter, parents are allotted ample credit *and* criticism no matter who they are.

Also, none of this discussion comes from a place of judgment; it comes from a place of learning. Though I'm not a parent myself (OK, I am a cat mom), I have two wonderful parents who raised me, and I have other kinds of parents, too, so I'm speaking on my experiences with them and those I see on TV. Parenting is A LOT of hard work, and there are many times when the right decision feels like the wrong one at the time. Just like no one is a perfect person, no one is a perfect parent.

Lane's relationship with Mrs. Kim is one of the other mother-daughter duos with which the viewers are most familiar. Like Emily, Mrs. Kim has hard-and-fast rules. No getting up to go to the bathroom while everyone is still eating. No TV. No boys. No French fries, a.k.a. the devil's starchy fingers. And oh, yeah–no boys.

Lane fights against these boundaries every chance she gets. She has towers of makeup and a library of CDs hidden underneath her bedroom floorboards. She has a disco-closet hideout when she needs to escape from her mother. She secretly scarfs down pizza when Mrs. Kim buys okra in bulk on the internet. Obviously, these two do not see eye to eye. Even when Lane tries to bargain with Mrs. Kim to be able to play in the band and still adhere to the Kim house rules, Mrs. Kim refuses and kicks Lane out.

However, the tables turn when Lane grows up, marries Zack, and discovers that they're pregnant with twins. This time, when Mrs. Kim jumps into protective overdrive mode, it's to take care of Lane during her pregnancy. Mrs. Kim does the grocery shopping, reminds Lane to take prenatal vitamins, and even wants to move in with them. It may annoy Lane to have Mrs. Kim around so much, but Mrs. Kim is doing all this because she loves her daughter and is excited for her grandchildren.

They do have a major fight about whether Lane's kids will eat shrimp or whether they'll go to church, but Lorelai brokers peace, showing that sometimes, a godmother is exactly the parent one needs.

Lorelai has always ensured that Lane has food to eat, can see concerts and plays with Rory, and has a safe place to have emotional Judy Blume moments about touching a boy's hair. She even alters Mrs. Kim's wedding dress so Lane can wear it for her wedding. Lorelai has definitely been a parent to Lane over the years, providing a counterbalance to the strict Kim household. As the pièce de résistance, when Lane is put on bed rest and can't attend her baby shower, Lorelai decides to move the entire party to Miss Patty's and helps roll Lane's bed across the street and up the ramp just so that Lane can still have her baby shower. Though Lorelai was never officially recognized as godmother, as she was for Sookie's kids, Lane still sees her this way, and in honor of that relationship, she asks Rory to be the "Lorelai" to her own kids, Steve and Quan.

And it all comes full circle. Rory steps into the godmother shoes, and Lane adopts some of Mrs. Kim's state of mind for her kids. Lane was so intent on having the baby shower because, in her mind, that would be her last party. She realizes that Mrs. Kim did everything for her, and she wants to do the same for her kids. Lane even gives up going on tour with Vapor Rub with Zack to stay with her children, and I'm guessing she also chooses Steve and Quan over putting her energy into making Hep Alien more successful. Influenced by Mrs. Kim's outlook on parenting, Lane chooses her own version of motherhood.

When it comes to devotion, I have parents like Lorelai, Mrs. Kim, and Lane. I read in *The View from Down Here* that the author's dad carried her up several flights of stairs every day so she could make it to and from her internship. Similarly, when Rory starts to freak out about being an international news reporter without her mommy, Lorelai says that she would drop everything and learn to operate a camera so that she'll always be around to help Rory. As drastic as these examples sound, I know parents who would do that. I have those parents, and I am so blessed. While my father has never had to carry me up a flight of stairs every day,

I'm pretty sure he would. He *has* moved me across the country TWICE, and I've already detailed the incredible devotion my mother has shown while caring for me. The "celebration" for my most recent birthday included my dad installing blackout shades in my apartment and my mom helping me do multiple loads of laundry. All I have to do is call their name, and they'll be there on the next plane.

In Rory's Chilton graduation speech, she says Lorelai "never gave me any idea that I couldn't do whatever I wanted to do or be whomever I wanted to be." My parents did the same for me. I was a kid who came up with a copious amount of big ideas, and I'm still that person. When I came to my parents with extraordinary decisions such as running the Chicago Marathon, even though I'm not a runner, they were immediately on board and made sure I had ample stock of energy gels and Brazil nuts. When I told my parents I wanted to go to art school in a faraway city so I could write books, they supported my decision. They've moved me from Chicago to LA to New York and never, not once, told me I was being unrealistic, that my dreams were too big, or that I should focus on something practical like "business" that would be sure to make me money. So many of my classmates shared that their parents thought they were totally *Cuckoo's Nest* for trying to break into artistic industries that are notoriously hard to join and often pay very little. Every time I heard someone describe their unsupportive parents, I sent a mental "thank-you" to mine.

My parents have shaped who I am even when they don't realize it. There are days when I'll say something like, "I have five books planned (in my head) over the next ten years," and my mom will look at me and say, "Sometimes I don't know how you turned out to be you. It certainly didn't come from me." That conversation always feels like a Gilmore moment, like Lorelai, who didn't graduate high school, in awe of her daughter, who was accepted into three Ivy League universities.

I've said in those discussions with my mom, and I'll say it again here: "I am this way because you let me." I am who I am because my parents always supported my dreams. While my parents have helped in more ways than I can name here, they also gave me the structure to go after my dreams myself. They weren't going to do it for me, but they taught me to work hard for what I wanted.

My dad has planned major events for the automotive industry for his entire career, but the one thing I remember most about his job is how much he loved it. Now, I don't get cars, I hate driving, and even riding in one can make me physically sick. So much of what my dad has told me about his job completely baffles me, but I've always wanted to do something I loved, just like he does. My dad is also a big believer in the idea that if you don't ask, you'll never know, which always annoyed me as a kid because I was and am very introverted. But if I wanted to write a book, I'd have to ask a whole bunch of people (agents, publishers, illustrators, etc.) to be a part of my team. Many said no, but some said yes, and well, here you are, reading my book, so clearly, my dad's lessons paid off.

My creativity also came from both of my parents in indirect ways, like Lorelai influenced Rory even when she didn't realize it. My mom helped produce and direct many of our church's plays and theatrical events and directed the youth choir for years. One of my favorite things to do was sing in the car with my mom to one of our favorite songs, belting out our respective parts of the duet. My dad has played the trumpet in his band for years and always helped the bass and tenor sections of the youth choir to hear their parts. I grew up internalizing my parents' passion and dedication to creativity.

There are many talented, creative, passionate people in the world, but I've learned that endurance can be the difference between making it and leaving your dreams behind. It took me ten years after graduation from college to get a book deal, and as much as it would have killed me, I would have given this dream decades more. My parents gave me the foundation of creativity and the work ethic to do anything and everything I could to achieve my goals, no matter how long it took.

Most of my parents' rules reinforced that very lesson. As a kid, I didn't love doing chores like emptying the dishwasher. I wasn't a fan of budgeting with my allowance, and I definitely wanted to eat out more than cook food at home. But it all prepared me to do the work when it came down to it. It taught me to save what I have now for a bigger payout in the future, to sacrifice something small now so I can go after the big things later.

Lorelai, the Gilmores, and Mrs. Kim have opposite philosophies on child-rearing, but I think together they have the best impact. Structure and play. Parent and friend. As with many things in life, it's all a balance. Sometimes we get it right, and sometimes we don't. Plus, as much as our parents give us, one person can't be everything to us all the time; we need someone else to fill the other parental roles. That's why I think we need a combination of many parents so that we can encounter all the experiences, advice, and ways of living that we need to shape us as we grow.

When we meet Luke, he's a total bachelor. In the later seasons, he discovers he has a daughter, April, and scrambles to adjust to fatherhood. He stumbles a bit, being a little too clingy on the field trip, buying April a toiletry kit for her birthday, and deciding to hang out in a park when it's freezing outside, but he eventually finds his way—much like Miles in *Empire Falls*. As much as April and Luke come to love each other, I think Luke's most significant parental impact is not with his own child.

First, there was Rory. He baked her special coffee cakes for her birthday, always gave her a gift (a unicorn something or monogrammed towels), and was vehemently protective about Rory when it came to her dating life. When Rory gets into a car accident with Jess, he tells Lorelai he cares about Rory more than he does himself. His love for Rory and his reaction to her leaving Yale prompted Lorelai to propose to Luke in season six. Luke was all in, including seeing Rory as his daughter. He was the bridge between Rory and Lorelai during their fight and always encouraged Rory to stay true to her goals. Rory did need a father figure in her life; her biological father had a tough time getting his act together, but she had that father in Luke—and so did Jess.

Jess came to Stars Hollow an angry, messed-up teenager with no sense of responsibility, communication, or purpose. Luke wasn't sure what to do with his surly nephew, but he did provide structure, ensuring

Jess went to school and worked at the diner. The cantankerous diner owner also provided some much-needed tough love, animatedly encouraging Jess to attend his mother's wedding and leading by example in learning how to communicate effectively. It may have taken years for the lessons to sink in, but eventually, Jess became the man he did because of Luke's steadfast perseverance.

There are so many kinds of parents in our lives, and all have an effect on us. Growing up, we had a close-knit group of girlfriends who would always visit one another's homes on a rotating basis. Because we were there so much, we started considering each other's parents our pseudo-parents. I haven't seen many of them in years, but I still think of them in a parental manner. Just as friends come in and out of our lives, sometimes parents do too. At my previous job, I considered one colleague my "work mom." She took me out to dinner every year for my birthday and was always there if I needed to talk. She also knew that my mom lived far away and couldn't do everyday mother-daughter things like going to the doctor with me for moral support, so she volunteered to do that as well. I don't see her like I used to, but I know that if I picked up the phone today and asked her to come to a doctor's appointment, she would, which is why I still consider her my work mom. She and all the other parents who have come and gone in my life still hold a special place in my heart. They were all there at a time when I needed them and have had a lasting impact on me in one way or another, helping to shape who I am today.

You never know who your kid will grow up to be. Mrs. Kim certainly didn't think she'd have a rock 'n' roll–loving daughter, but that's why it's important to have an entire community's worth of influences and examples. One person can't be everything to everyone all the time. In an *It Takes a Village* kind of way, kids need rules and flexibility, structure and fun, facts and imagination, a friend and a parent. The best way to experience this is to have different kinds of parents in many other places—just like everyone in Stars Hollow played a different parental role for Rory and Lane. So, take in the lessons that all your "parents" have taught you and use that wisdom to help you grow. You may not even realize how they've helped to shape who you are, but give it a few years, and you'll start to see the signs. And when you have someone in your life who has shown you the kindness of love, remember to thank them for their influence and for the monogrammed towels.

Thanks for being my Lorelai, Gilmore.

Behind the Scenes: Lauren Teaching Alexis How to Work on a TV Set

Moms are there to lend a helping hand or, in this case, an arm to pull you in the right direction. *Gilmore Girls* was the first big acting gig for Alexis Bledel, so she wasn't in the habit of certain things that are part of an actor's job, like hitting your mark. Many *Gilmore* scenes required walk-and-talks, extended depictions of the actors strolling through Stars Hollow with the spitfire dialogue they became known for. To help Alexis during these scenes, Lauren would link arms with her and practically drag her to each of their marks. On-screen, it reinforces the idea of the closeness of Lorelai and Rory's relationship, but it's actually Lauren looking out for her TV daughter, Alexis.

Keiko Agena and Emily Kuroda: Lane and Mrs. Kim in Real Life

We all love hearing stories about cast and crew who are good friends on and off set. That's why *Gilmore* fans love the special relationship between Emily Kuroda (Mrs. Kim) and her TV daughter, Lane, played by Keiko Agena. Since the show ended, the pair have been teaming up for events and reunions, and we can't get enough. Their adventures include a reading of *Girl Taking Over: A Lois Lane Story* for a book launch, attending plays like *Unrivaled*, and taking part in a reading of the play *Yamaguchi Store,* giving fans a *Gilmore* combo that will always fill our hearts with joy.

Dear Universe, More Gilmore, Please

When Good Things Come to an End

"There are just a lot of things right now in my life that are undecided, and that used to scare me, but now I kind of like the idea that it's just all kind of . . . wide open."

—Rory (Sn 7 Ep 21)

Gilmore Girls aired its final season in 2007, and although Netflix gave us the four-part miniseries in 2016, *Gilmore Girls: A Year in the Life*, the years between watching the Gilmores on our screens have felt like an eternity. We all love Lorelai and Rory, and more time with them is always amazing, but there are a lot of fans with mixed feelings about *A Year in the Life*, and I understand why. Sometimes, when something is so magical the first time around, it's hard to keep all that magic alive over so many years and reproduce it exactly. Though the creators and cast have a "never say never" attitude about reuniting to film more episodes, there may never be an end to the *Gilmore* drought we're experiencing now. Therefore, I'd like to manifest more *Gilmore* in the world–and not just the world at large but in my own world too.

This chapter is dedicated to bringing about all the *Gilmore* goodness: not just another TV show but also other *Gilmore* opportunities in the days ahead. The *Gilmore* fan community is the best, and I love being a part of it, so I want to bring more Stars Hollow into being for them if I can. I'm sure my passion for having more *Gilmore Girls* doesn't surprise anyone. After all, you've just read an entire *Gilmore* celebration, so let's get more *Gilmore*!

More Gilmore for the World

Prequel Shows

This is a big one: I'm manifesting a *Gilmore* prequel show. It's the perfect way to have your cake and eat it too. You wouldn't need the original cast, so there would be no scheduling issues or raising people from the dead. Plus, the fans wouldn't assign their feelings about the previous cast to the new one (hopefully), so it's a sort of new beginning.

One prequel would focus on Lorelai Gilmore, the first of that name, in her college or early adult years with her husband and raising a young Richard. Trix is such a phenomenal character, but we don't get to spend as much time with her as we do with Richard and Emily, so Trix's contribution to the Gilmore legacy is still relatively unknown. Most of her fame comes from stories her relatives tell about her, but a show of her own gives Trix her time to shine. Aren't you curious about how she fell in love and decided to marry her second cousin, all her travels, her upbringing and relationship with her parents, and her relationship with Richard when he was young? So. Many. Questions!

The other prequel would focus on college-age Richard and Emily. All of Richard's hijinks at Yale like wearing only a bow tie and nothing else or tossing his roommate out the window every night. Emily showing up at that party in the blue dress to steal him away from Pennilyn Lott. Richard in the Whiffenpoofs (I did the whole *Pitch Perfect* a capella thing in high school, so this would be a big part of the show for me). And then Emily and Richard getting married (for the first time), going on their honeymoon, and starting their new life together. And, of course, soon comes baby Lorelai. I mean, would you not binge-watch the bejesus out of this? I know I would!

True Love for Rory

This one contrasts a little with the previous manifestation request because it requires some kind of sequel to *AYITL*. Would I watch a *Gilmore* sequel? Yes. Would I count down the days and binge-watch it the second it was released? Yes. Would I also be really nervous about what I was about to see? Also yes. Part of the frustration of *AYITL*, in my opinion, was Rory's love life.

Rory deserves more. Rory should demand more. More than what's-his-name that everyone always forgets and more than a man who's cheating on his wife and/or fiancée with her. Whether that ends up being Jess, which I know a lot of people want and I'd be totally on board with, or some new guy who has the Luke and Lorelai magic, Rory should have someone who is always there for her, who loves her, who supports her, who is her best friend and partner.

Gilmore Festivals and Celebrations

One of the biggest parts of the *Gilmore* fandom is exactly that: the fans. I've met (online and in person) so many wonderful *Gilmore Girls* fans. Bonding with them over our favorite quotes, characters, and moments is so, so special.

Gilmore fans are some of the best in the world, and I believe a part of that is because we've repeatedly internalized all these *Gilmore* lessons every time we watch the show. I have loved connecting with honorary Gilmores, and I look forward to more amazing events where I can meet you and share in all that *Gilmore* goodness.

Amy Sherman-Palladino/Lauren Graham Rewatch Podcast

I know ASP is a busy woman, and podcasting isn't exactly the kind of thing she does, but a rewatch podcast with her would be endlessly fascinating and instantly successful. True, there are plenty of rewatch podcasts out there, and Scott Patterson has given fans a nice behind-the-scenes look with his own, but I want to hear it from the iconic ASP herself. She is the one with "much knowledge" about everything from the initial idea, dialogue, writing the scripts, show direction, costumes, directors, actors, and so much more. Maybe even with Daniel Palladino as her cohost? Of course, they'd have access to every single cast and crew member from the show to give all the behind-the-scenes details and incredible memories and anecdotes.

If the Palladinos are too busy, which I totally understand, my other choice is the witty embodiment of Lorelai Gilmore herself, Lauren Graham. Her books have an incredible conversational style that would be perfect for podcasting, and I'm sure, based on her granny impressions and Ephronistic style, she'd be an absolute hoot to listen to, but she'd be able to pull off the emotional moments so well too. Lauren has revealed in interviews that Mae Whitman, Lauren's *Parenthood* daughter, has wanted them to team up for a podcast; obviously, this would be amazing, too, and I'm sure some *Gilmore* stories would naturally come out of such a podcast. Mae–I'm on your side; get Lauren to host a podcast!

For anyone who's wondering (and even if you're not), I'd be happy to be a guest on this podcast at any time. Or to help ASP write or show-run if she needed a helping hand for another sequel or a prequel. Let this essay stand as a résumé and informal interview for all the powers that be to consider me as a writer/guest/host for these projects. I'm even up for portraying Luke's Patron #4 in a series reboot!

Really. I'll be waiting. Just. Call. My. Name. I'll be there. On the next train.

OK, you get it, call me

More Gilmore Food

So far, I've listed several opportunities for more *Gilmore* that I really have no control over. However, despite my almost Gilmore lack of cooking skills (I *can* stir to combine, thank you very much), Gilmore food is the one thing I can help with. I'm going to keep buying Pop-Tarts and having pizza on a weekly basis, but I've used my *Gilmore* connections to bring a little Stars Hollow to all of you. My friend Larisa has created another *Gilmore*-inspired recipe just for you.

EMILY GILMORE'S HOMEMADE TWINKIES

INGREDIENTS:

For the Twinkies:

¼ cup heavy cream
⅓ cup shortening
⅔ cup granulated sugar
3 eggs
1 tsp vanilla
¼ tsp salt
2 tsp baking soda
1 cup flour

For the filling:

½ cup heavy cream
½ cup powdered sugar
1 cup marshmallow fluff
½ tsp vanilla
1 tsp cream of tartar

DIRECTIONS:

1. Preheat the oven to 350°F and grease the wells of a Twinkie mold. If you don't have a Twinkie mold, you could alternatively use a 9x13-inch baking dish and cut the cake into bars.
2. In a large mixing bowl, cream together the heavy cream, shortening, and sugar.
3. Add in one egg at a time, mixing in between. Then add in the vanilla and salt.
4. Sift in the baking soda and flour and mix until fully combined.
5. Carefully pour the batter into the wells of the Twinkie mold. Fill the wells only about halfway. My pan had wells of 4.5x1.8 inch and this recipe makes 8.

6. Bake at 350°F for 15-20 minutes or until the cakes are golden brown and an inserted toothpick comes out clean.
7. Allow the cakes to cool completely.
8. Prepare the filling by adding the heavy cream and powdered sugar to a large mixing bowl. Using an electric mixer, whip the cream and sugar until stiff peaks form.
9. Add in the marshmallow fluff, vanilla, and cream of tartar and whisk until combined. Keep refrigerated until ready to use.
10. Once the cakes have cooled, use the base of a metal piping tip or paring knife to cut 3 holes in the bottom of each cake. The hole should be about ½ inch in diameter and go about ¾ of the way to the top of the cake.
11. Transfer the filling to a piping bag and pipe the filling into the holes. Once you notice the cake start to give, press the tip of the piping bag into the filling slightly to help prevent the filling from oozing back out.

More Gilmore for Me

Friday Night Dinners

Rory tells Lorelai that the Friday Night Dinners are important to her because it's the only time during the week that the entire family gets together. There's something I really love about that too. I didn't always have friends or family nearby after I moved away from home, so I understand how Rory feels, especially when I'm experiencing a flare and it's more difficult for me to go out. So, one night when everyone I love is gathered would be the perfect social fix for the week.

In today's busy world, it can be hard to juggle everyone's schedule and bring people together, so a weekly dinner might be the best solution—you always know it's on your calendar. And the FND (Friday Night Dinner) doesn't have to be on Friday nights; maybe a Sunday brunch is more the group's style! Of course, it would be close family and friends, but if they had a friend in town or started dating someone or there's a new person in the office, they could come too. Like a weekly Friendsgiving! New York can be a tough place to find your people, but I think this would really help.

Even hosting the dinner isn't mandatory for a FND! Currently, I don't even have a table to eat at, so I need to either move, find someone else to host, eat out every week, or everyone gets comfortable having a picnic in my living room. And I'm not cooking. I barely like cooking when I'm feeling well, but on the 50/50 chance that I'm sick for a FND, cooking is completely out of the question. However, there were two FNDs on *Gilmore Girls* where they ate frozen pizza, so that seems doable. I'll figure out all the details at some point. See you Friday night for dinner!

Emily and Rory Take Europe

The Gilmores sure know how to travel! I'm happy to do the Rory and Lorelai Europe vacation too; I just know I wouldn't be able to sustain the backpacking portion of the trip. I'm older now and have already done the hostel thing in college. I've worked excruciatingly hard to get to where I am, and I have multiple chronic illnesses, so I don't think it's too much to ask to be able to travel in style like Emily at least once in my life. Bonus points for traveling in style to more than one country in Europe. I'd also really love a European Christmas market trip. Can you imagine all the shopping Emily could do during the holidays? Or at the couture houses in Paris? Extra bonus points for a luxury trip to Asia, South America, Australia, Africa, Antarctica, and the remaining states in the US that I haven't yet visited. I know Emily probably doesn't care much about these (see her feelings on Richard's trip to Ohio), but it's on my bucket list, and I'm going to tempt her with spa trips (clearly, she'll drive to North Carolina to visit a spa) and rare manuscript sightings (hey, she bought a table for the rare manuscript foundation fundraiser, so she has to go). Bon Voyage!

Cast and Crew Quotes on the *Gilmore Girls* 25th Anniversary

Lauren Graham (Lorelai Gilmore) on *Second Home* Podcast

"It's really a time for incredible gratitude that I got to be part of something that is meaningful for people, especially something that is of comfort to people and a source of happiness . . ."

Stan Zimmerman (Writer)

"As we celebrate the twenty-fifth anniversary of the premiere of *Gilmore Girls*, I'm reminded of the party for the two-hundredth episode. First there was a small gathering onstage for cake and pictures. Then there was a big evening party at a restaurant in West LA. Both of these events were highly unusual, since we didn't get to mingle much with the cast and crew. We were always locked away in the writers' room at the bungalow across the Warner's lot. We would see the cast at the weekly table reads, but I was usually in panic mode because ASP had me read the stage directions. I never wanted to jump in at the wrong place and ruin the snappy flow of the scenes. It was a dance that Lauren and I would just fall naturally fall into. Kelly and Ed were most often on a voice box, since they were still back east. These readings would take place a few days before filming of that episode began. This would give us time to rewrite. I am forever grateful for my brief stint on *Gilmore Girls*. I grew in so many ways. And met so many amazing people. And continue to as the legacy of the series seems to keep growing, Stars Hollow forever!"

Emily Kuroda (Mrs. Kim)

"*Gilmore Girls* has been a gift that keeps on giving. I have met four generations who have been touched by the honesty, love, and humor of this genius show. My hat's off to Amy Sherman-Palladino and Dan Palladino. I am so very grateful to have been a part of the Stars Hallow magic."

Michael Winters (Taylor Doose)

"Given the opportunity of thinking back over seven glorious seasons in Stars Hollow, I am awash with nostalgia for a wonderful time–many episodes like the dance marathon, the corn maze, the Revolutionary War reenactment in the snow, sleigh rides around the square, a political campaign–and so many more. Getting to play with so many splendid people–Lauren and Alexis, Melissa and Ted, Keiko, Sean, Milo, Matt, and on and on. Getting to meet Carole King–that fantastic impromptu song fest in Miss Patti's dance studio after a full day of a shooting, ceaselessly hassling Scott, hanging out with George Bell, the script guru: all the terrific material and guidance from Amy and Daniel.

But in the end, I think the greatest times I had were with Sally Struthers and Liz Torres, two grand, generous, funny, and dear ladies. Liz and I spent many, many hours together overseeing all those town meetings, much of the time sitting on the dais, tossing out cues for the rest of the company while they were being filmed. Between takes we happened on our own version of 'Name That Tune.' One would just start singing some classic old saloon song. When they couldn't come up with the next lyric, the other would–or we'd both work till we got it, or it was time for the next take . . . some pretty fond memories . . ."

Sebastian Bach (Gil)

"Wherever I go on tour around the world people are watching the Gilmore girls! The show truly has an international life of its own! I love being a part of the show and always remember: Without Gil it would just be *More Girls*!"

Todd Lowe (Zack)

"What I didn't foresee at the time, but thoroughly appreciate now, is the staying power the show has had. I've met three, possibly four, generations of fans who know the series backward and forward."

Rini Bell (Lulu)

"Being a citizen of Stars Hollow and living in that little world was a pure pleasure. I look back on my time as Lulu and feel really delighted with the experiences I got to have as her, the people I got to know, and the world I got to live in. It felt safe, important, human, and adorable."

Devon Michaels (Bill)

"As *Gilmore Girls* approaches its silver jubilee, I'm reminded that moment of connection it's produced–from the briefest recognition at a coffee shop to the forging of deep friendships at fan fests–is a testament to the unique feeling of family the show created for so many. It's humbling and gratifying to be part of such a uniquely enduring source of warmth and comfort. I've had other triumphs, and expect more in the future, but it's hard to imagine any bringing quite the same sense of having had, as Bill himself might say, 'a ringside seat for the [television] event of the century.'"

EPILOGUE

Unto the Breach

Lorelai: "I just feel like I need more time."
Rory: "Mom, you've given me everything I need."

—(Sn 7 Ep 22)

How do you move on from something that has changed your life "impermeably and forever"? How does one step out of the whimsical world of *Gilmore Girls* and back into the real world? I knew I'd have to answer these questions when I reached the end of writing *Meet Me at Luke's,* and I wasn't looking forward to it. *Gilmore Girls* has been my comfort show, my safe space for so long, and moving on is unfathomable.

However, the ironic beauty of this conundrum is that you don't have to move on at all! You can keep saying, "You're a Vicious Trollop" and reading *The Legend of Bagger Vance* and *The Electric Kool-Aid Acid Test* from the Rory Gilmore Reading Challenge. You can read or listen to this book and Lauren Graham's books as often as you want, and Netflix, hopefully, will keep *Gilmore Girls* available for streaming because we deserve to binge-watch and rewatch to our heart's content, always craving one more trip back to Stars Hollow.

The incredible part about reexperiencing any art form is that your perception of it changes every time. Take viewers' connections to different *Gilmore* characters, for example. So many fans who grew up with the show related to Rory, but as they watch it now, they're more in tune with Lorelai—and there's an excellent explanation for that. There are many versions of this quote, but Robertson Davies, author of *The Manticore*, said, "You can never read the same book twice." There is so much going on in our bodies and minds and our world that we are in a constant state of change. Even if the change is imperceptible, when you return to a book or a TV show, you are effectively a different person with a different point of view. And how you connect with and interpret that piece of art will be slightly altered from your original opinion. Even though this book and *Gilmore Girls* will essentially stay the same each time, your personal growth will change their messages. You will be bringing these stagnant pieces of art into the future with you, adapting them to the lifestyles of our current world.

When I started planning this book, I already knew some of the lessons I wanted to include from the *Gilmore Book Club* blog. However, as is the case with many journeys, there were lessons I'd learned that I had no concept of before taking every single step of this journey, lessons that I didn't even know I needed to learn.

Savor

I've spent countless hours listening to podcasts, interviews, and audiobooks on *Gilmore Girls* and other popular TV shows and films, and nearly everyone has commented on how fast these incredible experiences (like making a TV show) tend to fly by. That's an extraordinary feat, considering how slowly some individual moments tick along. From one day to the next, it's everything at once or nothing, a

roller coaster you desperately want to exit but, for many reasons, can't bring yourself to leave. It's why Lauren Graham has no idea where "oy with the poodles" came from and why Alexis can't remember the origins of "copper boom." In all the chaos, especially when you have a copious number of lines to remember, your brain steps in and wipes the slate clean so you can keep functioning. This process may save you in some instances, but in others, you find yourself aghast at the moments of your life that replay in your brain like TV static.

It's always struck me as tremendously sad to hear of all the moments from some of our time's most iconic pop culture sensations where the people involved can recall only a handful of memories. Forgetting so much of the journey is the one thing I promised myself I'd avoid whenever I got my shot at "the big time." Of course, just like Rory gets distracted by finding a replacement map instead of taking in the big moment of moving into her Yale dorm for the first time, I let the daily chores and frustrations distract my mind from the big picture of the entire book-writing experience. In *Gilmore Girls*, Lorelai is there to take the map from Rory's hand and demand that she be in the moment. It's a redo that's certainly worth it, because Rory takes some time to appreciate how hard she's worked to be at Yale and the exciting new journey she is about to undertake.

My mom and my friend Andrea have acted as my Lorelais here, congratulating me on each step I take and reminding me to always take inventory of my feelings and appreciate how far I've come since I started the publishing process. However, my mom and BFF aren't with me on a daily basis, so each time I work on this book, it's up to me to remember the importance of savoring each moment.

I've been successful and unsuccessful in savoring the experience of writing my first book. My phone has selfies stored of my outfits and smiles after my first meetings with my agent and editor and the times my cat, Cleo, has jumped on my lap to offer her company as I sat at my desk to write this book. I've kept all the different versions of the sketches my illustrator has sent me so I can look back on where we started. Someday, I'll put all of those plus some odds and ends into a scrapbook and do my best to write down how I was feeling and what I was thinking during this process.

I wish I had done better at taking notes or writing in my journal as I went along; I'm sure there are valuable things that have already slipped my mind, and I'll be able to recover only some of them when I go back over everything. It's not perfect, and it's not complete, but I've given it my best. The lesson of "savoring" all the big and small moments that make up our lives is perhaps one of the most important lessons I've discovered during my *Gilmore Girls* immersion, and I want to ensure that I take that knowledge with me into whatever project I take on next.

I hope you commit to savoring the vicissitudes of life in your own way. Sometimes you'll have someone to help remind you, like when Richard takes over the photography responsibilities at Rory's Yale graduation and reminds Lorelai to savor the moment of her daughter getting her diploma. However, you may not always be surrounded by a gaggle of Gilmores, so the responsibility to savor will often fall to you–don't let yourself forget! Take pictures, write things down, leave yourself voice notes, collect coasters or pins, make scrapbooks or photobooks, or whatever floats your boat and doesn't turn your home into an episode of *Hoarders*. Keep those memories to remind yourself of all the little moments in your life that made you who you are. Savor the past, the present, and the hope of the future.

Hopefully, I've now put you in the mood to savor, because I am about to recap every delicious morsel of The Perks of Being a Gilmore, and I want you to relish every bite. I know, I know, we've been here before (do you recognize that tree?), but it always helps to look at where you've been before you move forward to ensure you take all that wisdom you've gained into your future endeavors so your life doesn't become *A Comedy of Errors*.

Meet Me at Luke's, in addition to being a celebration of *Gilmore Girls,* is my attempt to answer the all-important question: What would a Gilmore do? The Gilmore mindset is something fans strive to achieve, and I, too, aim for more *Gilmore* in my life. I wrote this book to illustrate specific lessons but also to portray the general ways to be like a Gilmore. The good news is that these Gilmorean doctrines do not involve buying expensive Venetian apples like Emily; rather, they're the tenets that the characters of *Gilmore Girls* have shown that they live by and value, and they are wonderfully accessible and doable.

A true Gilmore does the hard work: they do their research, they look at the deeper meaning, and they ask all the questions. They open their minds to everything this world has to give, deciding what works for them and what to put aside. A Gilmore is also genuine, living life on their own terms. So, don't be afraid to Gilmorify your life; decide what you want and go after it, cast out what doesn't serve you, and never stop questioning, learning, and growing. That is a Gilmore through and through.

Just as Lorelai and Rory change and grow throughout the show's seven seasons, so have we learned new things about ourselves and the world through the pages of *Meet Me at Luke's*. We've examined the necessity of showing up in all kinds of relationships (parent-child, friendships, and romances). Yes, communication is key, but you have to be willing to put your money where your mouth is. (Sorry, Doyle, was that too many clichés?) *Meet Me at Luke's* has also helped us identify our purpose, get out of our own way, and stay true to ourselves. These subjects take a lot of dedication and hard work, which we also know is needed for creating your home and community. We've also cultivated creativity from literature, traveling, and music—remember, inspiration is all around you! We approached the difficulties in life like health, wellness, money, and gratitude. Throughout these chapters, we have also celebrated the passion and perseverance of Amy Sherman-Palladino and other iconic women from history and pop culture. I sincerely hope that through all this, we've manifested more *Gilmore* in the world.

One of the main topics I have discussed with *Gilmore Girls* fans is their love for the show's strong sense of community. I've had the pleasure of meeting wonderful people who love this series, and I know I'll encounter many more who feel like instant friends because of our *Gilmore* connection. I'm so grateful for the wide variety of people within

the fandom. I've heard stories from peers and colleagues who, for some reason or other, missed the show when it was on cable but are now, thanks to streaming, discovering Stars Hollow and falling in love with its residents. I have had family members tell me they're bingeing the show so they can fully be a part of the fun fandom when this book comes out. And without fail, one out of every ten conversations with my mom will contain a story about how she discovered that her hairdresser, coworker, or friend at church is a major *Gilmore* fan. I'm never surprised at these connections, and I love each time our little corner of the world gains a new member. These people are from all over the world, have different ethnicities and backgrounds, and are of varying ages with varying interests and yet *Gilmore Girls* unites us all.

This beloved show has a unique quality to transform itself to be precisely what the viewer needs at that moment. And the *Gilmore* fandom has an exquisite way of making it their own. It's evident in my blog and everyone participating in the Rory Gilmore Reading Challenge. It's clear in the content creators, like Larisa, who generously provided this book's recipes and is baking all the iconic treats from the show. That outlook is also visible in the opinions of those I think of as the next generation of *Gilmore* fans. Since they weren't around to see the show in its original form and context, it's fascinating to hear their point of view, how they treasure this world without the pressures of social media and the tight-knit community that is such a rarity these days, how they question Rory's decisions—fully aware of the internet rants about how Rory lost her way and whether her aimlessness could affect them—how watching

a world where fax machines and dial-up internet is a cozy, nostalgic vacation they couldn't experience anywhere else.

Between the original audience and the new generation of fans, there are so many people who've benefitted from this show and are part of making the world a better, more Gilmore place. I hope you've found the same joy and comfort in *Meet Me at Luke's* as you have in *Gilmore Girls* and will carry that with you to whatever comes next. I hope the time spent analyzing Lorelai and Rory, Paris and Lane, Emily and Richard, and everyone else has given you something to think about, something to ignite personal growth, something to comfort you, and something to inspire you. Because the best part about being a Gilmore is being *your* version of a Gilmore.

Go forth and Gilmore!

APPENDIX

The Rory Gilmore Reading Challenge Book List Checklist

Get ready to embark on the reading challenge of a lifetime! If you're ready to read like a Gilmore, here's the list of all the literature shown or mentioned by any character on the show.

A few tips:

- Please don't put too much pressure on yourself to read everything in a year; take your time and enjoy it.
- Take a break from a difficult or triggering book when you need to.
- Read how you read best: listen to the audiobook or read a hard copy. If watching the movie first helps you better understand the book, then do that!
- Read books about the culture of a specific period (Shakespeare, Dickens, Austen, etc.) to help you acclimate better when reading the book.
- Talk to your friends, listen to book podcasts, watch YouTube book reviews–anything that gives you a different perspective on the literature to help you think about these books.

If you want a digital reading tracker that counts books you have read and allows you to sort this list by author, subject, or GG character, check out the *Gilmore Book Club Deluxe Reading Tracker* here.

Titles with an 🎬 are also movies listed on the Gilmore Movie Challenge list. (For the full movie challenge list, visit gilmorebookclub.com.)

1984 by George Orwell (1949) 🎬
A Bolt from the Blue and Other Essays by Mary McCarthy (2002)
A Brief History of Time by Stephen Hawking (1988) 🎬
A Christmas Carol by Charles Dickens (1843) 🎬
A Clockwork Orange by Anthony Burgess (1962) 🎬
A Comedy of Errors by William Shakespeare (1589–94, pub. 1623) 🎬
A Confederacy of Dunces by John Kennedy Toole (1980)
A Connecticut Yankee in King Arthur's Court by Mark Twain (1889)
A Heartbreaking Work of Staggering Genius by Dave Eggers (2000)
A Mencken Chrestomathy by H. L. Mencken (1949)
A Midsummer Night's Dream by William Shakespeare (1600) 🎬
A Monetary History of the United States by Milton Friedman (1963)
A Month of Sundays: Searching for the Spirit and My Sister by Julie Mars (2005)
A Moveable Feast by Ernest Hemingway (1964)
A Passage to India by E. M. Forster (1924) 🎬
A Quiet Storm by Rachel Howzell Hall (2002)
A Room of One's Own by Virginia Woolf (1929)
A Room with a View by E. M. Forster (1908) 🎬
A Separate Peace by John Knowles (1959) 🎬
A Streetcar Named Desire by Tennessee Williams (1947) 🎬
A Tale of Two Cities by Charles Dickens (1859) 🎬
A Tree Grows in Brooklyn by Betty Smith (1943) 🎬
A Version of Love by Millicent Dillon (2003)
Alice's Adventures in Wonderland by Lewis Carroll (1865) 🎬
All the Pretty Horses by Cormac McCarthy (1992) 🎬
An American Tragedy by Theodore Dreiser (1925)
And Then There Were None by Agatha Christie (1939) 🎬
Angela's Ashes by Frank McCourt (1996) 🎬
Animal, Vegetable, Miracle: A Year of Food Life by Barbara Kingsolver (2007)

Anna Karenina by Leo Tolstoy (1878) 🎬
Anne Frank: The Diary of a Young Girl by Anne Frank (1947) 🎬
As I Lay Dying by William Faulkner (1930) 🎬
Atonement by Ian McEwan (2001) 🎬
Autobiography of a Face by Lucy Grealy (1994)
Babe by Dick King-Smith (1983) 🎬
Backlash: The Undeclared War against American Women by Susan Faludi (1991)
Balzac and the Little Chinese Seamstress by Dai Sijie (2000) 🎬
Being There by Jerzy Kosinski (1970) 🎬
Bel Canto by Ann Patchett (2001) 🎬
Beloved by Toni Morrison (1987) 🎬
Beowulf: A New Verse Translation by Seamus Heaney (2000) 🎬
Bitch: In Praise of Difficult Women by Elizabeth Wurtzel (1998)
Brave New World by Aldous Huxley (1932)
Breakfast at Tiffany's by Truman Capote (1958) 🎬
Brian's Song by William Blinn (1971) 🎬
Brick Lane by Monica Ali (2003) 🎬
Bridgadoon by Alan Jay Lerner (1947) 🎬
Call Me Crazy by Anne Heche (2001)
Candide by Voltaire (1759)
Carrie by Stephen King (1974) 🎬
Catch-22 by Joseph Heller (1961)
Charlie and the Chocolate Factory by Roald Dahl (1964) 🎬
Charlotte's Web by E. B. White (1952) 🎬
Christine by Stephen King (1983) 🎬
"Cinderella" by Charles Perrault (1697) 🎬
Clifford the Big Red Dog by Norman Bridwell (1967) 🎬
Collected Poems, 1934–1953 by Dylan Thomas (2003)
Collected Short Stories by Aldous Huxley (1957)
Complete Stories by Dorothy Parker (1995)
Counterpoint by Roy Newquist (1964)
Cousin Bette by Honoré de Balzac (1846) 🎬

Crime and Punishment by Fyodor Dostoevsky (1866)
Cujo by Stephen King (1981)
Daisy Miller by Henry James (1879)
Daughter of Fortune by Isabel Allende (1998)
David Copperfield by Charles Dickens (1850)
Dead Souls by Nikolai Gogol (1842)
Death of a Salesman by Arthur Miller (1949)
Deenie by Judy Blume (1973)
Demons by Fyodor Dostoevsky (1872)
Divine Secrets of the Ya-Ya Sisterhood by Rebecca Wells (1996)
Doctor Faustus by Christopher Marlowe (1604)
Don Quixote by Cervantes (1605 and 1615)
The Strange Case of Dr. Jekyll and Mr. Hyde by Robert Louis Stevenson (1886)
Dracula by Bram Stoker (1897)
Driving Miss Daisy by Alfred Uhry (1987)
Dumbo the Flying Elephant by Helen Aberson-Mayer and Harold Pearl (1941)
Eleanor Roosevelt by Blanche Wiesen Cook (1992, 2000, and 2016)
Ella Minnow Pea: A Novel in Letters by Mark Dunn (2001)
Eloise by Kay Thompson (1955)
Emily the Strange by Roger Reger (2002)
Emma by Jane Austen (1815)
Empire Falls by Richard Russo (2001)
Encyclopedia Brown: Boy Detective by Donald J. Sobol (1963)
Ethan Frome by Edith Wharton (1911)
Ethics by Baruch Spinoza (1677)
Elements by Euclid (c. 300 BCE)
Europe through the Back Door by Rick Steves (2003)
Eva Luna by Isabel Allende (1987)
Every Man in His Humor by Ben Jonson (1598)
Everything Is Illuminated by Jonathan Safran Foer (2002)
Extravagance by Gary Krist (2002)

Fahrenheit 451 by Ray Bradbury (1953) 🎬
The Official Fahrenheit 9/11 Reader by Michael Moore (2004) 🎬
Fat Land: How Americans Became the Fattest People in the World by Greg Critser (2003)
Fathers and Sons by Ivan Turgenev (1862)
Fear and Loathing in Las Vegas by Hunter S. Thompson (1971) 🎬
Fiddler on the Roof by Joseph Stein (1964) 🎬
Finding Time Again (In Search of Lost Time, book 7) by Marcel Proust (1927)
Finnegan's Wake by James Joyce (1939)
Firestarter by Stephen King (1980) 🎬
Fletch by Gregory Mcdonald (1974) 🎬
Flowers for Algernon by Daniel Keyes (1966) 🎬
Flowers in the Attic by V. C. Andrews (1979) 🎬
Forty Days by Bob Simon (1992)
Frankenstein by Mary Shelley (1818) 🎬
Franny and Zooey by J. D. Salinger (1961)
Freaky Friday by Mary Rodgers (1972) 🎬
Galápagos by Kurt Vonnegut (1985)
Gender Trouble by Judith Butler (1990)
George W. Bushisms: The Slate Book of Accidental Wit and Wisdom of Our 43rd President by Jacob Weisberg (2001)
Gidget by Fredrick Kohner (1957) 🎬
Girl, Interrupted by Susanna Kaysen (1993) 🎬
Global Woman: Nannies, Maids, and Sex Workers in the New Economy by Barbara Ehrenreich (2003)
Goldilocks and the Three Bears by Alvin Granowsky (1988)
Gone with the Wind by Margaret Mitchell (1936) 🎬
Great Expectations by Charles Dickens (1860) 🎬
Gulliver's Travels by Jonathan Swift (1726) 🎬
Hamlet by William Shakespeare (1603) 🎬
"Hansel and Gretel" by the Brothers Grimm (1812) 🎬
Harold and the Purple Crayon by Crockett Johnson (1955) 🎬
Harry Potter and the Goblet of Fire by J. K. Rowling (2000) 🎬

Harry Potter and the Sorcerer's Stone by J. K. Rowling (1997)

Heart of Darkness by Joseph Conrad (1899)

Helter Skelter: The True Story of the Manson Murders by Vincent Bugliosi and Curt Gentry (1974)

Henry IV, Part 1 by William Shakespeare (1596–97)

Henry IV, Part 2 by William Shakespeare (1597–98)

Henry V by William Shakespeare (1599–1600)

Henry VI by William Shakespeare (1589–92)

He's Just Not That into You by Greg Behrendt and Liz Tuccillo (2004)

High Fidelity by Nick Hornby (1995)

Holidays on Ice by David Sedaris (1997)

House of Sand and Fog by Andre Dubus III (1999)

How the Grinch Stole Christmas by Dr. Seuss (1957)

How the Light Gets In by M. J. Hyland (2003)

How to Breathe Underwater by Julie Orringer (2003)

Howl and Other Poems by Allen Ginsberg (1956)

I'm with the Band by Pamela Des Barres (1987)

Idioglossia by Mark Handler (1985)

In Cold Blood by Truman Capote (1966)

In the Shadow of Young Girls in Flower (In Search of Lost Time, book 2) by Marcel Proust (1919)

Indiana by George Sand (1832)

Inherit the Wind by Jerome Lawrence and Robert E. Lee (1955)

Ironweed by William J. Kennedy (1983)

It Takes a Village by Hillary Clinton (1996)

Jane Eyre by Charlotte Brontë (1847)

Julius Caesar by William Shakespeare (1599–1600)

Just a Couple of Days by Tony Vigorito (2001)

Kitchen Confidential: Adventures in the Culinary Underbelly by Anthony Bourdain (2000)

Lady Chatterley's Lover by D. H. Lawrence (1928)

Larousse Encyclopedia of Wine by Christopher Foulkes (1994)
Lassie Come-Home by Eric Knight (1940) 🎬
Leaves of Grass by Walt Whitman (1855)
Less Than Zero by Bret Easton Ellis (1985)
Letters of Ayn Rand edited by Michael Berliner (1995)
Letters to a Young Poet by Rainer Maria Rilke (1929)
Lies and the Lying Liars Who Tell Them by Al Franken (2003)
Life of Pi by Yann Martel (2001)
Like Water for Chocolate by Laura Esquivel (1992) 🎬
Lisa and David by Theodore Isaac Rubin, MD (1961) 🎬
Little Dorrit by Charles Dickens (1857) 🎬
Little House on the Prairie by Laura Ingalls Wilder (1935) 🎬
Little Red Riding Hood by Charles Perrault (1697) 🎬
Little Women by Louisa May Alcott (1868) 🎬
Living History by Hillary Clinton (2003)
Lolita by Vladimir Nabokov (1955) 🎬
Lord Jim by Joseph Conrad (1900) 🎬
Lord of the Flies by William Golding (1954) 🎬
Love Medicine by Louise Erdrich (1984)
Love Story by Erich Segal (1970)
Macbeth by William Shakespeare (1623) 🎬
Madame Bovary by Gustave Flaubert (1856) 🎬
Madeline by Ludwig Bemelmans (1939) 🎬
Main Street by Sinclair Lewis (1920)
Marathon Man by William Goldman (1974) 🎬
Mary Poppins by P. L. Travers (1934) 🎬
Master and Commander by Patrick O'Brian (1969) 🎬
Me Talk Pretty One Day by David Sedaris (2000)
Memoirs of a Dutiful Daughter by Simone de Beauvoir (1958)
Memoirs of General W. T. Sherman by William T. Sherman (1886)
Men Are from Mars, Women Are from Venus by John Gray (1992)
Middlesex by Jeffrey Eugenides (2002)
Misery by Stephen King (1987) 🎬

Moby-Dick by Herman Melville (1851)
Molière: A Biography by Hobart Chatfield Taylor (1906)
Molloy by Samuel Beckett (1951)
Monsieur Proust by Céleste Albaret (1973)
Mrs. Dalloway by Virginia Woolf (1925)
Mutiny on the Bounty by Charles Nordhoff and James Norman Hall (1932)
My Lai 4: A Report on the Massacre and Its Aftermath by Seymour M. Hersh (1970)
My Life as Author and Editor by H. L. Mencken (1993)
My Life in Orange: Growing Up with the Guru by Tim Guest (2004)
My Man Jeeves by P. G. Wodehouse (1919)
My Name Is Aram by William Saroyan (1940)
My Sister's Keeper by Jodi Picoult (2004)
Myra Waldo's Travel and Motoring Guide to Europe, 1978 by Myra Waldo (1978)
Naked Lunch by William S. Burroughs (1959)
Nervous System: Or, Losing My Mind in Literature by Jan Lars Jensen (2004)
New Poems of Emily Dickinson by Emily Dickinson (1993)
Nicholas Nickleby by Charles Dickens (1839)
Nickel and Dimed by Barbara Ehrenreich (2001)
Night by Elie Wiesel (1956)
Northanger Abbey by Jane Austen (1817)
Notes of a Dirty Old Man by Charles Bukowski (1969)
Novels 1930–1942 and *Novels 1944–1962* by Dawn Powell (2001)
Of Human Bondage by W. Somerset Maugham (1915)
Of Mice and Men by John Steinbeck (1937)
Old Christmas by Washington Irving (1876)
Old School by Tobias Wolff (2003)
Oliver Twist by Charles Dickens (1838)
On Death and Dying by Elisabeth Kübler-Ross (1969)
On the Road by Jack Kerouac (1957)

One Day in the Life of Ivan Denisovich by Aleksandr Solzhenitsyn (1962) 🎬
One Flew Over the Cuckoo's Nest by Ken Kesey (1962) 🎬
One Hundred Years of Solitude by Gabriel García Márquez (1967)
Oracle Night by Paul Auster (2003)
Oryx and Crake by Margaret Atwood (2003)
Othello by William Shakespeare (1603) 🎬
Our Mutual Friend by Charles Dickens (1865) 🎬
Out of Africa by Isak Dinesen (1937) 🎬
Paper Moon by Joe David Brown (1971) 🎬
Paradise Lost by John Milton (1667)
"Paul Revere's Ride" by Henry Wadsworth Longfellow (1861)
Peter and Wendy by J. M. Barrie (1911) 🎬
Peyton Place by Grace Metalious (1956) 🎬
Pigs at the Trough by Arianna Huffington (2003)
The Adventures of Pinocchio by Carlo Collodi (1883) 🎬
Pippi Longstocking by Astrid Lindgren (1945) 🎬
Please Kill Me: The Uncensored Oral History of Punk by Legs McNeil and Gillian McCain (1996)
Points of View by W. Somerset Maugham (1958)
Pride and Prejudice by Jane Austen (1813) 🎬
Primary Colors by Joe Klein (1996) 🎬
Property by Valerie Martin (2003)
Pushkin: A Biography by T. J. Binyon (2002)
Pygmalion by George Bernard Shaw (1912) 🎬
Quattrocento by James McKean (2002)
"R" Is for Ricochet by Sue Grafton (2004)
Rapunzel by the Brothers Grimm (1812)
Reading Lolita in Tehran: A Memoir in Books by Azar Nafisi (2003)
Rebecca by Daphne du Maurier (1938) 🎬
Rebecca of Sunnybrook Farm by Kate Douglas Wiggin (1903) 🎬
Rescuing Patty Hearst: Memories from a Decade Gone Mad by Virginia Holman (2003)
Rita Hayworth and the Shawshank Redemption by Stephen King (1982)

Robert's Rules of Order by Henry Robert (1876)
"Roman Fever" by Edith Wharton (1934)
Romeo and Juliet by William Shakespeare (1597) 🎬
Rosemary's Baby by Ira Levin (1967) 🎬
Rotten: No Irish, No Blacks, No Dogs by John Lydon (1994)
"S" Is for Silence by Sue Grafton (2005)
Sacred Time by Ursula Hegi (2003)
Sadako and the Thousand Paper Cranes by Eleanor Coerr (1977)
Samuel Johnson: The Major Works by Samuel Johnson (1925)
Sanctuary by William Faulkner (1931)
Savage Beauty: The Life of Edna St. Vincent Millay by Nancy Milford (2001)
Save Me the Waltz by Zelda Fitzgerald (1932)
Schindler's List by Tomas Keneally (1982) 🎬
Seabiscuit: An American Legend by Laura Hillenbrand (1999) 🎬
Secrets of the Flesh: A Life of Colette by Judith Thurman (1999)
Selected Letters of Dawn Powell: 1913–1965 by Dawn Powell (1999)
Sense and Sensibility by Jane Austen (1811) 🎬
Sexus by Henry Miller (1949)
Shakespeare's Sonnets by William Shakespeare (1609)
Shane by Jack Schaefer (1949) 🎬
Siddhartha by Hermann Hesse (1922) 🎬
Slaughterhouse-Five by Kurt Vonnegut (1969) 🎬
Small Island by Andrea Levy (2004)
Snow-White and Rose-Red by the Brothers Grimm (1837) 🎬
Social Origins of Dictatorship and Democracy: Lord and Peasant in the Making of the Modern World by Barrington Moore Jr. (1966)
Sodom and Gomorrah (In Search of Lost Time, book 4) by Marcel Proust (1921)
Song of the Simple Truth: The Complete Poems of Julia de Burgos by Julia de Burgos (1997)
Songbook by Nick Hornby (2002)
Sonnets from the Portuguese by Elizabeth Barrett Browning (1850)
Sophie's Choice by William Styron (1979) 🎬

Speak, Memory by Vladimir Nabokov (1951)
Stiff: The Curious Lives of Human Cadavers by Mary Roach (2003)
Stuart Little by E. B. White (1945) 🎬
Sula by Toni Morrison (1973)
Swann's Way (In Search of Lost Time, book 1) by Marcel Proust (1913)
Swimming with Giants: My Encounters with Whales, Dolphins and Seals by Anne Collet (2000)
Sybil by Flora Rheta Schreiber (1973)
Tender Is the Night by F. Scott Fitzgerald (1934) 🎬
Terms of Endearment by Larry McMurtry (1975) 🎬
The Adventures of Huckleberry Finn by Mark Twain (1884) 🎬
The Adventures of Tom Sawyer by Mark Twain (1876) 🎬
The Age of Innocence by Edith Wharton (1920) 🎬
The Amazing Adventures of Kavalier & Clay by Michael Chabon (2000)
The Apocalyptics: Cancer and the Big Lie by Edith Efron (1984)
The Archidamian War by Donald Kagan (1974)
The Art of Eating by M. F. K. Fisher (1954)
"The Art of Fiction" by Henry James (1884)
The Art of War by Sun Tzu (475–221 BCE)
The Awakening by Kate Chopin (1899)
The Bell Jar by Sylvia Plath (1963) 🎬
The Bhagavad Gita (c. 200–100 BCE)
The Bible (1000 BCE–200 CE)
The Bielski Brothers: The True Story of Three Men Who Defied the Nazis, Built a Village in the Forest, and Saved 1,200 Jews by Peter Duffy (2003) 🎬
The Canterbury Tales by Geoffrey Chaucer (1387–1400) 🎬
The Cask of Amontillado by Edgar Allan Poe (1846) 🎬
The Catcher in the Rye by J. D. Salinger (1951)
"The Celebrated Jumping Frog of Calaveras County" by Mark Twain (1865)
The Children's Hour by Lillian Hellman (1934) 🎬
The Code of the Woosters by P. G. Wodehouse (1938)

The Collected Stories of Eudora Welty by Eudora Welty (1980)
The Complete Poems by Anne Sexton (1981)
The Complete Tales & Poems of Edgar Allan Poe by Edgar Allan Poe (1849)
The Count of Monte Cristo by Alexandre Dumas (1844) 🎬
The Crimson Petal and the White by Michel Faber (2002)
The Crucible by Arthur Miller (1953) 🎬
The Curious Incident of the Dog in the Night-Time by Mark Haddon (2003)
The Da Vinci Code by Dan Brown (2003) 🎬
The Defender of the Peace by Marsilius of Padua (1324)
The Devil in the White City: Murder, Magic, and Madness at the Fair that Changed America by Erik Larson (2003)
The Diary of Virginia Woolf edited by Anne Olivier Bell (1977)
The Dirt: Confessions of the World's Most Notorious Rock Band by Neil Strauss, Vince Neil, Nikki Sixx, Mick Mars, Tommy Lee (2001)
The Divine Comedy by Dante (1320)
The Duchess of Malfi by John Webster (1614)
The Electric Kool-Aid Acid Test by Tom Wolfe (1968)
"The Eve of Waterloo" by Lord Byron (1816)
The Executioner's Song by Norman Mailer (1979)
The Fair Penitent by Nicholas Rowe (1703)
The Fall of the Athenian Empire by Donald Kagan (1987)
The Fellowship of the Ring by J. R. R. Tolkien (1954) 🎬
The Five People You Meet in Heaven by Mitch Albom (2003) 🎬
The Fortress of Solitude by Jonathan Lethem (2003)
The Fountainhead by Ayn Rand (1943) 🎬
The Frog Prince by the Brothers Grimm (1812) 🎬
The Fugitive (In Search of Lost Time, book 6) by Marcel Proust (1925)
The German Quarter by Lev Nitoburg (1933)
The Gettysburg Address by Abraham Lincoln (1863)
The Gnostic Gospels by Elaine Pagels (1979)
The God of Small Things by Arundhati Roy (1997)
The Godfather by Mario Puzo (1969) 🎬
The Good Soldier by Ford Madox Ford (1915) 🎬

The Good Life by Jay McInerney (2006)
The Graduate by Charles Webb (1963) 🎬
The Grapes of Wrath by John Steinbeck (1939) 🎬
The Great Gatsby by F. Scott Fitzgerald (1925) 🎬
The Great Santini by Pat Conroy (1976) 🎬
The Group by Mary McCarthy (1963) 🎬
The Guermantes Way (In Search of Lost Time, book 3) by Marcel Proust (1920)
The History of the Decline and Fall of the Roman Empire by Edward Gibbon (1776–1789)
The Holy Barbarians by Lawrence Lipton (1959)
The House of the Spirits by Isabel Allende (1982) 🎬
The Hunchback of Notre Dame by Victor Hugo (1831) 🎬
The Iliad by Homer (c. 800 BCE)
The Interpretation of Dreams by Sigmund Freud (1899)
The Joy Luck Club by Amy Tan (1989) 🎬
The Jungle by Upton Sinclair (1906)
The Kitchen Boy: A Novel of the Last Tsar by Robert Alexander (2003)
The Kite Runner by Khaled Hosseini (2003) 🎬
The Last Empire: Essays 1992–2000 by Gore Vidal (2001)
The Last Lion: Winston Spencer Churchill by William Manchester and Paul Reid (vol. 1: 1983, vol. 2: 1988, vol. 3: 2012)
The Legend of Bagger Vance by Steven Pressfield (1995) 🎬
The Lion, the Witch and the Wardrobe by C. S. Lewis (1950) 🎬
The Little Locksmith by Katharine Butler Hathaway (1943)
The Little Match Girl by Hans Christian Andersen (1845) 🎬
The Lost Weekend by Charles R. Jackson (1944) 🎬
The Lottery and Other Stories by Shirley Jackson (1949) 🎬
The Lovely Bones by Alice Sebold (2002)
The Magic Mountain by Thomas Mann (1924) 🎬
The Man in the Gray Flannel Suit by Sloan Wilson (1954)
The Man without Qualities by Robert Musil (1930)
The Manticore by Robertson Davies (1972)

The Mark of Zorro by Johnston McCulley (1919) 🎬
The Master and Margarita by Mikhail Bulgakov (1967) 🎬
The Meaning of Consuelo by Judith Ortiz Cofer (2003)
The Merchant of Venice by William Shakespeare (1600) 🎬
The Merry Wives of Windsor by William Shakespeare (1597) 🎬
The Metamorphosis by Franz Kafka (1915)
The Miracle Worker by William Gibson (1959) 🎬
The Mojo Collection: The Ultimate Music Companion by Jim Irvin (2001)
The Mourning Bride by William Congreve (1679)
The Naked and the Dead by Norman Mailer (1948) 🎬
The Name of the Rose by Umberto Eco (1980) 🎬
The Namesake by Jhumpa Lahiri (2003) 🎬
The Nanny Diaries by Emma McLaughlin (2002)
The New Way Things Work by David Macaulay (1988)
The Norton Anthology of Theory and Criticism by William E. Cain, Laurie A. Finke, Barbara E. Johnson, John P. McGowan, and Jeffrey J. Williams (2001)
Odyssey by Homer (c. 800 BCE)
The Opposite of Fate: Memories of a Writing Life by Amy Tan (2003)
The Outbreak of the Peloponnesian War by Donald Kagan (1969)
The Outsiders by S. E. Hinton (1967) 🎬
The Peace of Nicias and the Sicilian Expedition by Donald Kagan (1981)
The Perks of Being a Wallflower by Stephen Chbosky (1999)
The Picture of Dorian Gray by Oscar Wilde (1891) 🎬
The Poetry of Robert Frost by Robert Frost (1969)
The Polysyllabic Spree by Nick Hornby (2004)
The Portable Dorothy Parker by Dorothy Parker (1944)
The Portable Nietzsche by Friedrich Nietzsche (1954)
The Power and the Glory by Graham Greene (1940) 🎬
The Power of Myth by Joseph Campbell and Bill Moyers (1988) 🎬
The Price of Loyalty: George W. Bush, the White House, and the Education of Paul O'Neill by Ron Suskind (2004)
The Prince by Niccolò Machiavelli (1532)

The Princess Bride by William Goldman (1973) 🎬
The Prisoner (In Search of Lost Time, book 5) by Marcel Proust (1923)
The Raven by Edgar Allan Poe (1845) 🎬
The Razor's Edge by W. Somerset Maugham (1944) 🎬
The Real Animal House by Chris Miller (2006) 🎬
The Red Badge of Courage by Stephen Crane (1895) 🎬
The Red Tent by Anita Diamant (1997)
The Republic by Plato (401)
The Return of the King by J. R. R. Tolkien (1955) 🎬
The Rough Guide to Europe, 2003 Edition (2003)
The Scarecrow of Oz by L. Frank Baum (1915)
The Scarlet Letter by Nathaniel Hawthorne (1850) 🎬
The Second Sex by Simone de Beauvoir (1949)
The Secret Life of Bees by Sue Monk Kidd (2001)
The Secret of the Old Clock (Nancy Drew Series #1) by Carolyn Keene (1930)
The Shadow of the Wind by Carlos Ruiz Zafón (2001)
The Shining by Stephen King (1977) 🎬
The Silence of the Lambs by Thomas Harris (1988) 🎬
"The Snows of Kilimanjaro" by Ernest Hemingway (1936) 🎬
The Song of Names by Norman Lebrecht (2002)
The Song Reader by Lisa Tucker (2003)
The Sound and the Fury by William Faulkner (1929) 🎬
The Story of Doctor Dolittle by Hugh Lofting (1920) 🎬
The Story of My Life by Helen Keller (1903) 🎬
The Sun Also Rises by Ernest Hemingway (1926) 🎬
"The System of Doctor Tarr and Professor Fether" by Edgar Allan Poe (1845) 🎬
"The Tell-Tale Heart" by Edgar Allan Poe (1843) 🎬
The Time Traveler's Wife by Audrey Niffenegger (2003)
The Tragedy of Richard III by William Shakespeare (1597) 🎬
The Trial by Franz Kafka (1925) 🎬
The True and Outstanding Adventures of the Hunt Sisters by Elisabeth Robinson (2004)

The Two Towers by J. R. R. Tolkien (1945) 🎬

The Unabridged Journals of Sylvia Plath 1950–1962 by Sylvia Plath (2000)

The Vanishing Newspaper by Philip Meyer (2004)

The Velvet Underground and Nico by Joe Harvard (2004)

The Virgin Suicides by Jeffrey Eugenides (1993) 🎬

The White Devil by John Webster (1612)

The Wisdom of the Ancients by Francis Bacon (1609)

The Witch Tree Symbol (Nancy Drew Series #33) by Carolyn Keene (1955)

The Wonderful Wizard of Oz by L. Frank Baum (1900) 🎬

The Year of Magical Thinking by Joan Didion (2005)

The Yearling by Marjorie Kinnan Rawlings (1938) 🎬

Time and Again by Jack Finney (1970)

To Have and Have Not by Ernest Hemingway (1937) 🎬

To Kill a Mockingbird by Harper Lee (1960) 🎬

Truth & Beauty: A Friendship by Ann Patchett (2004)

Tuesdays with Morrie by Mitch Albom (1997) 🎬

Tusculan Disputations by Cicero (45 B.C.E.)

Ulysses by James Joyce (1922)

Uncle Tom's Cabin by Harriet Beecher Stowe (1852) 🎬

Understanding Power by Noam Chomsky (2002)

Unfinished Business: Memoirs 1902–88 by John Houseman (2000)

Unless by Carol Shields (2002)

U.S.A. (*The 42nd Parallel, 1919,* and *The Big Money*) by John Dos Passos (1937)

Valley of the Dolls by Jacqueline Susann (1966) 🎬

Vanity Fair by William Makepeace Thackeray (1848) 🎬

Visions of Cody by Jack Kerouac (1972)

Waiting for Godot by Samuel Beckett (1953)

Walden by Henry David Thoreau (1854)

Walt Disney's Bambi by Felix Salten (1922) 🎬

War and Peace by Leo Tolstoy (1869) 🎬

We Owe You Nothing – Punk Planet: The Collected Interviews edited by Daniel Sinker (2001)

What Color Is Your Parachute? 2005 by Richard Nelson Bolles (2005)
What Ever Happened to Baby Jane? by Henry Farrell (1960) 
What to Expect When You're Expecting by Heidi Murkoff, Arlene Eisenberg, Sandee Hathaway (1984)
When the Emperor Was Divine by Julie Otsuka (2002)
Who Moved My Cheese? by Spencer Johnson (1998)
Who's Afraid of Virginia Woolf? by Edward Albee (1962) 
Who's Who and What's What in Shakespeare by Evangeline M. O'Connor (2000)
Wicked: The Life and Times of the Wicked Witch of the West by Gregory Maguire (1995)
Working: People Talk about What They Do All Day and How They Feel about What They Do by Studs Terkel (1974)
Written in Blood: The Story of the Haitian People 1492–1995 by Michael Heinl, Nancy Gordon Heinl, Robert Debs Heinl (1978)
Wuthering Heights by Emily Brontë (1847)

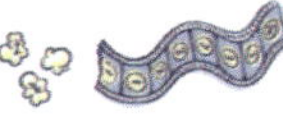

TV Shows Mentioned in Gilmore Girls

A Gilmore lifestyle would be incomplete without a plethora of television shows to watch and rewatch. Each show below was mentioned in a *Gilmore Girls* episode. These are a few of my favorites, but make sure to check out the full list on gilmorebookclub.com.

Bewitched (1964–1972)
Everybody Loves Raymond (1996–2005)
Fame (1982–1987)
Family Feud (1976–)
Gilligan's Island (1964–1967)
I Dream of Jeannie (1965–1970)

I Love Lucy (1951–1957)
Live with Regis and Kelly (now *Live with Kelly and Mark*) (2001–2011)
Powerpuff Girls (1998–2005)
Saturday Night Live (1975–)
Sex and the City (1998–2004)
SpongeBob SquarePants (1999–)
The Ed Sullivan Show (1948–1971)
The Oprah Winfrey Show (1986–2011)
The Sopranos (1999–2007)
The West Wing (1999–2006)

Movies Mentioned in Gilmore Girls

It's movie night—a classic Gilmore night of entertainment! You can use Rory's reading list to find all the books that have been adapted into movies. The complete Gilmore Movie Challenge List can be downloaded from this QR code or from the *Gilmore Book Club* blog home page.

Books the Gilmores Would Read Today

A Gilmore would never stop reading and learning! Check out gilmorebookclub.com for books that the characters of *Gilmore Girls* would be reading today to add to your #tbr (to be read list).

ACKNOWLEDGMENTS

Writing and binge-watching are often a solitary act, but like many works of art, publishing a book is the result of a team. *Meet Me at Luke's* has been in my heart and mind for so long, and I'm indebted to those who helped me put my heart on the page.

To my agent, Laura Mazer, who saw the potential of this book in its fledgling state and helped bring it to light. You've been a fantastic mentor, confidant, and advocate, for which I'll always be grateful.

To Laura Marr, my illustrator: You were an absolute dream to work with, interpreting all of my musings and spreadsheets into beautiful works of art. You did so much research on the show and me to give the fans *Gilmore* Easter eggs to find, and I'm so proud of what we created together. You made Stars Hollow real for all of us!

An enormous thank you to the team at Andrews McMeel: my editor, Katie Gould, whose *Gilmore* brainstorms helped take this book to the next level; Holly, who helped make this book so beautiful; Madison, Brianna, and Devon, whose meticulous proofing helped catch my mistakes; Riley, who helped share this book with the world; and all the sales people at Simon & Schuster. *Meet Me at Luke's* would not have been possible without all of you!

My deepest thanks to Kevin Treu, who read an early draft of this book. He reads everything from Stephen King to J. R. R. Tolkien and watches everything from Hallmark movies to Academy Award contenders. A fellow Gilmore brain, if ever there was one. Thank you for your detailed reading and thoughtful questions.

To Amy Sherman-Palladino and Daniel Palladino, Lauren Graham, Alexis Bledel, and Kelly Bishop, and all the *Gilmore Girls* cast and crew who sent in their quotes and supported this book in other ways, a gigantic thank you for sharing your experiences in the Gilmore family with me.

My journey to becoming an author wouldn't have been the same without the love and support of my friends and family. Mom, Dad, Jenny, and Andrea–thank you for all the calls, texts, hugs, and your unwavering faith in me.

To my Chronicon friends who have showered me with love and encouragement every step of the way. Your passion for books and steadfast community have meant the world to me. I consider it an honor and a job well done if this book gives the world even a fraction of the love and hope that you've given me.

To the fans, readers, booksellers, librarians, and Gilmores of all kinds, thank you for letting me into your hearts and onto your bookshelves.

ABOUT THE ILLUSTRATOR

After years as a designer and art director, Laura Marr could no longer resist her passion for illustration. She has since followed her heart, conjuring vibrant illustrations from her sunlit studio–and occasionally from airplanes, trains, and castles. Her love of travel, history, and nature radiates through her distinctive and vibrant work. In addition to client commissions, Laura also has a popular line of paper goods and gifts. Laura has created original artwork for a wide range of clients, including Capital One, Smithsonian Institution, Dover Publications, KEVA Style, Denik, and the Virginia Museum of Fine Arts. She has been an invited guest speaker at institutions such as the Art Institutes of America, RebelleCon, and the VCU School of Fine Arts. Most recently, her work was featured in the 2025 Society of Illustrators of Los Angeles Illustration West 63 Exhibition. Laura is represented by Greenwood Lit. You can explore more of her work on Instagram @flourishrva.

HARDWARE
Luke's
Luke's

Enjoy *Meet Me at Luke's* as an audiobook narrated by Stars Hollow's own Lane Kim, actress Keiko Agena, wherever audiobooks are sold.

The authorised representative in the EEA is Simon and Schuster Netherlands BV, Herculesplein 96 3584 AA Utrecht, Netherlands. (info@simonandschuster.nl)

Andrews McMeel Publishing
a division of Andrews McMeel Universal
1130 Walnut Street, Kansas City, Missouri 64106

www.andrewsmcmeel.com

25 26 27 28 29 VEP 10 9 8 7 6 5 4 3 2

ISBN: 979-8-8816-0085-3

Library of Congress Control Number: 2025935674

Editor: Katie Gould
Art Director: Holly Swayne
Production Editor: Brianna Westervelt
Production Manager: Julie Skalla

ATTENTION: SCHOOLS AND BUSINESSES
Andrews McMeel books are available at quantity discounts with bulk purchase for educational, business, or sales promotional use. For information, please email the Andrews McMeel Publishing Special Sales Department: sales@andrewsmcmeel.com.